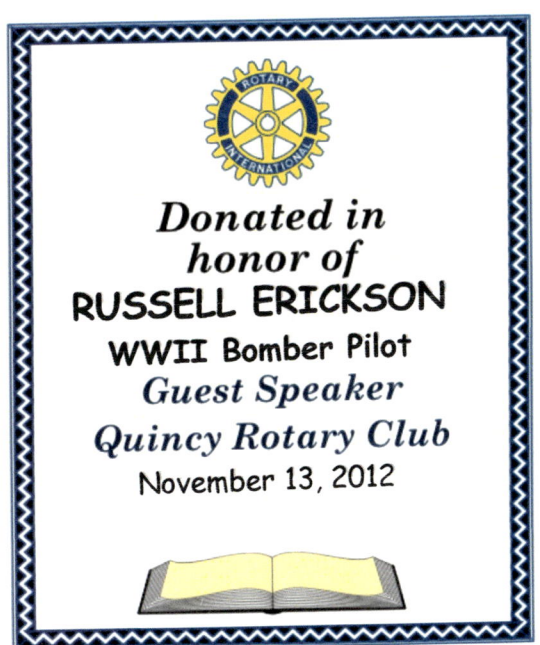

WORLD WAR II

WORLD WAR II BEGINS

Peter Darman, General Editor

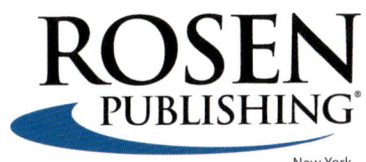

New York

This edition is published in 2013 by:

The Rosen Publishing Group, Inc.
29 East 21st Street, New York, NY 10010

Copyright © 2013 Brown Bear Books Ltd.

All rights reserved. No part of this book may be reproduced in any form without permission in writing from the publisher, except by a reviewer.

For Brown Bear Books Ltd:
Editorial Director: Lindsey Lowe
Senior Editor: Tim Cooke
Military Editor: Pete Darman
Children's Publisher: Anne O'Daly
Art Director: Jeni Child
Picture Manager: Sophie Mortimer

Library of Congress Cataloging-in-Publication Data

World War II begins/[editor] Peter Darman.
　　p. cm.—(World War II)
Includes bibliographical references and index.
ISBN 978-1-4488-9232-7 (library binding)
1. World War, 1939–1945—Causes—Juvenile literature. 2. Hitler, Adolf, 1889–1945—Juvenile literature. 3. Germany—Foreign relations—1933–1945—Juvenile literature. I. Darman, Peter. II. Title: World War Two begins.
D741.W664 2012
940.53'11—dc23

2012017543

Manufactured in the United States of America

CPSIA Compliance Information: Batch #W13YA: For further information, contact Rosen Publishing, New York, at 1-800-237-9932

Picture Credits:
All pictures: Robert Hunt Library
All artworks: Brown Bear Books

CONTENTS

Chapter 1  4

Adolf Hitler
The outbreak of World War II is closely tied to the ambitions Adolf Hitler had for Germany. Here we look at his character, his early life, and how World War I affected him. Then we examine his political beliefs, and how he organized the Nazi Party in the 1920s.

Chapter 2  14

Hitler's Rise to Power
Hitler's charismatic speech making earned him popular appeal among the German people. He became chancellor of Germany in 1933 and then established a centralized dictatorship.

Chapter 3  32

Europe in Crisis: 1935–1939
Many western European politicians were sympathetic to Hitler's aims in the early 1930s. However, by 1939 it became clear that his ambitions were to control the whole of Europe.

Chapter 4  48

Blitzkrieg in Poland
In September 1939 Hitler invaded Poland on a trumped-up pretext. The Poles resisted fiercely, but they were outgunned and finally stabbed in the back by a Soviet invasion from the east.

TIMELINE   SEPTEMBER 1939 – SEPTEMBER 1945   56

GLOSSARY   61

FURTHER READING   62

INDEX   63

CHAPTER 1
ADOLF HITLER

A failed artist and drop-out, Adolf Hitler would have been forgotten by history had it not been for the outbreak of World War I. In 1914 Hitler joined the German Army and fought on the Western Front. After the war he became involved in right-wing politics and discovered he had a talent for public speaking. Soon he became a national figure as head of the Nazi Party.

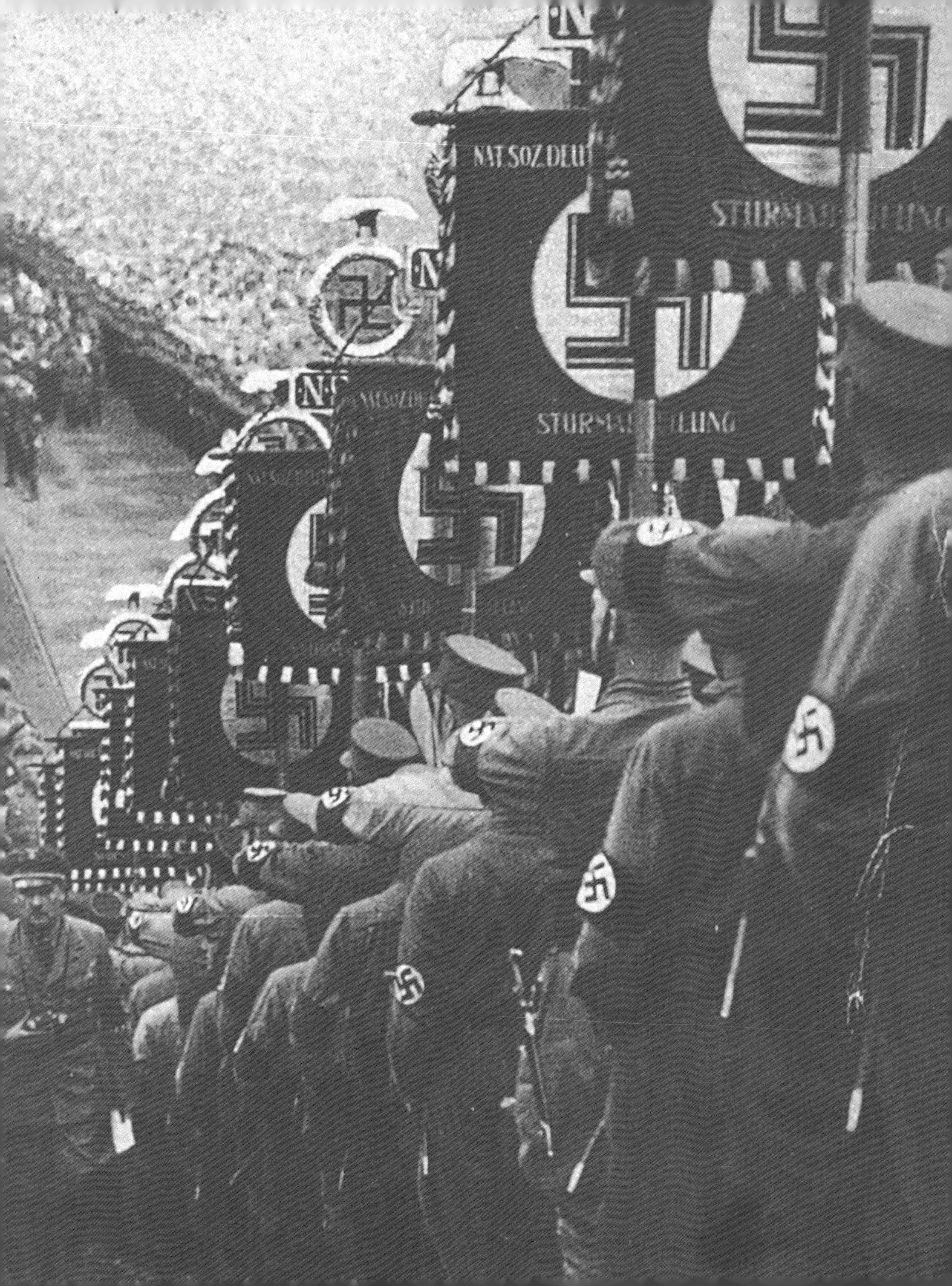
NAT. SOZ. DEU

Previous pages: Hitler at a mass Nazi rally in 1934.

Hitler in one of his "man of destiny" poses. The Nazis appreciated the advantages of the media, and used film and radio as tools to promote Hitler.

Like many Nazis, Adolf Hitler, born on April 20, 1889, came from Austria. He was also a misfit. His early years are well documented. He was born at Branau am Inn in Austria on the border with Germany in 1889, the son of an Austro-Hungarian customs official, Alois Hitler, aged 52, and a peasant girl, Klara Pölzl, some 30 years his junior. In 1876, Alois had changed his name from Schicklgruber to Hitler because the former sounded coarse and rustic. In this region of the Austro-Hungarian Empire, the names Hiedler, Hietler, Hüttler, Hütler, and Hitler, denoting "smallholder," were all used interchangeably. Alois was illegitimate, and Hiedler was the surname of his stepfather.

Hitler's childhood was not easy. While his mother doted on him, his father was a strict and difficult man and his use of physical punishment may well have had a profound impact on his son Adolf. From an early age, Adolf's strong will clashed with his father's, a clash that invariably led to the young Adolf being thrashed. As Adolf's younger sister Paula later remembered: "It was especially my brother Adolf who challenged my father to extreme harshness and who got his sound thrashing every day … How often, on the other hand, did my mother caress him and try to obtain with her kindness what my father could not succeed [in obtaining] with harshness."

Neither was Adolf's education a success. He performed poorly academically, was unruly, and was in constant trouble with teachers who attempted to control him. Hitler left school with an unbending dislike of schooling and teachers. This contempt for academic endeavor and all things intellectual would find its fullest expression in Nazism. The only subject that Hitler did find of interest during and after school was Germany: he soaked up books in the public library on all things German.

Life in Vienna

In 1907 Hitler went to Vienna where he attempted to enter the Vienna Academy of Fine Arts. However, he failed the entrance test—another blow to him and a further source for his hatred of teachers and intellectuals. The following year his mother died, and in the years afterward through to the outbreak of World War I Hitler eked out an existence in Vienna and Munich. The future chancellor of Germany was reduced to sleeping in rooming houses, and with his long overcoat, long hair, and unshaven appearance, fellow down-and-outs gave him the nickname of "Ohm Paul Krüger," after the Boer leader of the period. Hitler was, however, not the down-and-out he liked to subsequently portray. His standard of living improved with some handouts from his aunt, a legacy from his mother, and with the proceeds from his sketches, for which he could get five kronen per picture. At times his income was equivalent to that of a junior teacher; at other times he was short of money.

The traditional view is that Hitler developed his anti-Semitism in Vienna. However, it is not as clear cut as this. Many of the art dealers through whom Hitler sold his pictures were Jews. Hitler himself felt that the Jews he dealt with were better business people and more

Adolf Hitler

THE SPREAD OF COMMUNISM

In the aftermath of World War I, governments feared that Russia's Bolshevik revolution of 1917 would spread across Europe. They were concerned that workers in their own countries would convert to communism and attempt to overthrow the state. Bolsheviks, such as Lenin, followed the political theories of Karl Marx. He had argued that global revolution was an inevitable stage in human history. Exporting revolution was Bolshevik policy. In 1919, Soviet leaders founded the Communist International (Comintern) to coordinate communist parties around the world. One reaction was the "red scare" that swept the United States in 1919 and 1920. Many suspected communists were locked up or deported. The policy changed after Vladimir Lenin's death in 1924. His successor, Joseph Stalin, followed a program of "socialism in one country," or strengthening the revolution within the Soviet Union. Nevertheless the Comintern remained in being. All the governments of western Europe feared and distrusted the Soviet Union during the 1920s and 1930s, and this fear greatly helped Hitler.

reliable than the "Christian" dealers; he even struck up a good friendship with one Jewish dealer, Josef Neumann. However, Hitler later claimed in *Mein Kampf* that he became anti-Semitic after coming to Vienna from Linz. "Wherever I went, I began to see Jews, and the more I saw, the more sharply they became distinguished in my eyes from the rest of humanity." Hitler also began to associate Marxism with Jewry through what he called "the Jewish doctrine of Marxism."

Had war not broken out in 1914, Hitler would probably have eked out the rest of his life as a second-rate, obscure painter. But fate dictated otherwise.

Having joined the German army, Hitler now had a cause, comrades, and discipline. It was his first real job. He was desperate to stay with his regiment, the Bavarian Reserve Infantry Regiment 16 (known as the "List" Regiment after its commander), even after he had been wounded. Hitler later referred to the war years as "the greatest and most unforgettable time of my earthly life."

The future ruler of Germany spent the war as a dispatch runner, and never lacked for courage, although his superiors thought him lacking in leadership potential and he never rose above the rank of corporal. On December 2, 1914, Hitler was awarded the Iron Cross, Second Class. It was, he said, "the happiest day of my life." In the trenches, Hitler received few parcels from home; he neither smoked nor drank and he never visited brothels. Instead, he spent his time brooding or reading, the source of some amusement to his comrades, who mocked him for his seriousness. In the frontline, Hitler grew attached to Foxl, a small white terrier. Any affection that Hitler had amidst the horrors of the trenches was lavished on Foxl, and when the dog was lost Hitler was, for once, emotional. There were echoes here of Hitler's later attachment to his Alsatian dog Blondi.

> "Adolf challenged my father… and got his sound thrashing every day"

A portrait of Hitler's father, Alois. An exacting and unforgiving father, he died when Adolf was a boy. He is seen here with a Franz Joseph moustache and side-whiskers.

The famous shot of a jubilant Hitler in the Munich crowd following the outbreak of World War I. The future Nazi leader joined the German Army in 1914.

Wounded and decorated

In 1916 Hitler was wounded by a British shell and spent time in a hospital near Berlin. He was shocked to see the low morale and malingering behind the lines, and this image later provided the Nazis with their "Stab-in-the-Back" myth for why Germany lost the war. Hitler was eager to get back to the front, and so in March 1917 he rejoined the "List" Regiment near Vimy. On August 4, 1918, Hitler was awarded the Iron Cross, First Class, a rare distinction for an ordinary soldier in the Imperial German Army. Ironically, Hitler was nominated for the medal by a Jewish officer, Lieutenant Hugo Gutmann, for delivering a message through heavy fire. In October 1918, a month before the Armistice, Hitler was gassed with mustard gas and partially blinded. When the war ended he was convalescing in a hospital in Pomerania. The news of Germany's defeat shattered him. He recalled from his hospital bed how he "knew everything was lost. Only fools—liars or criminals—could hope for mercy from the enemy. In these nights my hatred grew against the men who had brought about this crime. I, however, decided to go into politics."

The Germany that Hitler returned to was being torn apart by a Left-versus-Right political battle as communists and right-wing paramilitary *Freikorps* units fought for control. As a devoted noncommissioned officer (NCO), Hitler was kept on the payroll of the "List" Regiment and given the task of spying on political parties in Munich. This represented his only proper peacetime employment with regular pay. It was one of these political parties that he was supposed to spy on, the German Workers' Party (*Deutsche Arbeiterpartei*, DAP), that attracted Hitler's attention most. In September 1919 the 30-year-old Hitler joined this party, as member 555,

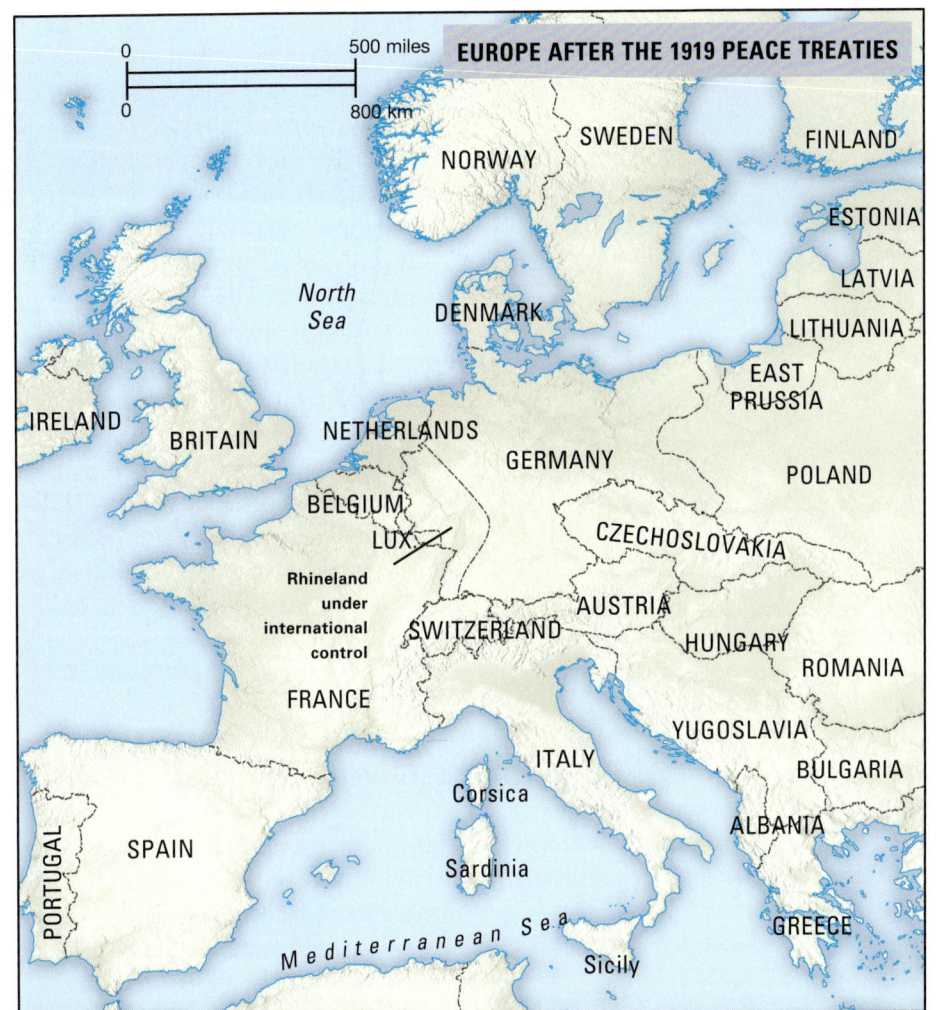

The map of Europe was transformed by the peace treaties that followed World War I. Germany was stripped of many territories and new nation states replaced earlier empires in central and eastern Europe.

German soldiers with Pickelhaube helmets and crude gas masks in the trenches in World War I. Hitler looked back fondly on his days on the Western Front.

although he later claimed he joined as member seven.

Hitler soon proved to be an excellent public speaker. His speeches attracted new members for the DAP, and in 1921 he moved to take over the party and give it a new name: the National Socialist German Workers' Party (*Nationalsozialistische Deutsche Arbeiterpartei*, NSDAP). This was shortened to the acronym "Nazi" from the first syllable of NAtional and the second syllable of SoZIalist. With the term "Nazi" came all the symbols of fascism that helped draw in new recruits. There were uniforms and a new greeting to replace *Guten Tag*: *Heil Hitler!* Eventually, school study periods

World War II Begins

An early Nazi Party meeting. The Nazi on the right wears an Iron Cross and the Swastika armband, an ancient symbol used by the Nazis.

in Germany were opened with "Heil Hitler!" and every child was expected to say "Heil Hitler!" over 100 times per day. Along with the greeting went the infamous raised right-arm salute. The Nazis also appropriated a powerful symbol in the Swastika (or *Hakenkreuz*). This was an ancient symbol that appeared on ceramics as far back as the fourth millennium BCE. Under the Nazis, the black Swastika on a white circular background against red came to denote the "superior" Aryan race. The Nazi propaganda machine under Dr. Josef Goebbels popularized the symbol as the official Nazi emblem.

The use of symbols and greetings was complemented by Hitler's program of simple political slogans backed up by the use of newspapers and Storm Troopers—the *Sturmabteilung* or SA, headed by another war veteran, the brutal Ernst Röhm—for battles on the streets with communists and social democrats. Hitler pushed the message that all Germany's woes were the result of international Jewry and Marxists, and his message was eagerly received by many in a population angered by the Treaty of Versailles and suffering from economic dislocation. Hitler's ideas of racial superiority and extreme nationalism were not new, but he colored them with showmanship and eloquence. Hitler certainly had a presence. When Hitler walked into a student cafe in Munich in 1921, Herbert Richter recalled: "He was

THE LEAGUE OF NATIONS

The League of Nations was the brainchild of U.S. president Woodrow Wilson. He intended it to resolve disputes between countries without warfare. The league was based on collective security. If one state threatened another, the members of the league would act together to stop the attacker. They would refuse to trade with it. As a last resort, they would take military action. The league came into being in 1919. Of its 44 founding members, 32 were Allied nations and 12 were neutral countries. None of the defeated powers was invited to join. Besides dealing with international disputes, the league had other duties. It governed the Saarland, part of the Rhineland in Germany. It also oversaw other territories taken from Germany and the Ottoman Empire. Those territories were governed under the mandate system. The league had some successes, but there was little it could do if a nation refused to cooperate. It was weakened by a number of factors. Powerful countries still preferred to solve their own problems, and in the 1930s they increasingly ignored the league. Some countries were not represented: Germany was only invited to join in 1926 and the Soviet Union in 1934. And, the greatest blow of all, the United States had refused to join. In 1946 the League was replaced by the United Nations.

wearing an open-necked shirt and he was accompanied by guards or followers … And I noticed how the people with whom he arrived—there were about three or four of them—how their eyes were fixed on Hitler. For many people there must have been something fascinating about him." Another contemporary recalled an encounter with Hitler: "Suddenly I noticed Hitler's eyes resting on me. So I looked up. And that was one of the most curious moments of my life. He didn't look at me suspiciously, but I felt that he was searching me somehow…. It was hard for me to sustain this look for so long. But I thought: I mustn't avert my eyes, otherwise he may think I've something to hide. And then something happened which only psychologists can judge. The gaze, which at first rested completely on me, suddenly went straight through me into the unknown distance. It was so unusual. And the long gaze which he had given me convinced me completely that he was a man with honorable intentions. Most people nowadays would not believe this. They'd say I'm getting old, but that's untrue. He was a wonderful phenomenon."

The "Beer Hall Putsch"

The creation of a "myth" around Hitler accelerated when, in 1923, he led an attempted coup (the so-called Beer Hall Putsch) in Munich as a prelude to a national revolution against the Weimar Republic. Again, all was not what it seemed at first sight. The putsch failed, and Hitler and the other ringleaders were put on trial in February 1924. Hitler stood up and claimed full responsibility for the putsch, which had claimed the lives of three policemen. His speech and behavior before the court made him known across Germany. He became a national figure.

> "The Storm Troopers fought battles on the streets"

Nazi storm troopers in 1923, the year of the "Beer Hall Putsch." These men, armed with rifles and truncheons, are mostly dressed in World War I-style clothing.

World War II Begins

FASCISM

Fascism rose to dominate Europe in the 1920s and 1930s. It spread in response to the growth of socialism, the threat of communist revolution, and the failure of liberal governments to secure political and economic stability after World War I. What we now call fascism was a mixture of very broad ideas. Various right-wing movements across Europe were able to adapt it to suit their countries' political conditions. It was characterized by nationalism, militarism, dictatorship, and political repression. Such qualities stood out against the democratic and internationalist ideals of the League of Nations. Fascism rejected democratic politics and the class struggle of communism. Instead it believed the state should be a single entity, run by a strong leader. The citizen owed loyalty to the state, and the state's future should be shaped by its pursuit of its traditional values.

Hitler in NSDAP uniform with fellow Nazi Gregor Strasser (fourth from right), 1927. Strasser eventually came to be seen as a threat to Hitler and was assassinated in 1934. ▼

Before the judges, Hitler proclaimed: "Gentlemen, it is not you who pronounce judgment upon us, it is the eternal court of history which will make its pronouncement upon the charge which is brought against us [high treason].... You may pronounce us guilty a thousand times, but the goddess who presides over the eternal court of history will, with a smile, tear in pieces the charge of the Public Prosecutor and the verdict of this court. For she acquits us."

Mein Kampf

Sentenced by a sympathetic judge to the minimum term of five years' imprisonment, Hitler served his sentence in a comfortable cell in Landsberg prison. He was out after 10 months, having written his manifesto while in prison. Hitler's original title for this manifesto was *Four and a Half Years of Struggle against Lies, Stupidity, and Cowardice*. This was reduced to the snappier *Mein Kampf* ("My Struggle") by Hitler's publisher, Max Amann (who was later to become President of the Reich Press Chamber). The turgid, rambling discussion in *Mein Kampf* has been seen by many as a blueprint for Hitler's later actions, although the pragmatic and reactive policies that

Hitler as demagogue. Hitler made much use of hand gestures to increase the effect of his speeches.

Hitler followed when in power suggest otherwise. Soon, however, every home in Germany had to have a copy of *Mein Kampf* (even if few Germans actually read it) and the royalties from sales of the book were the main source of Hitler's personal income.

Hitler and struggle

In the development of the Nazi state, Hitler's personality and ideas naturally played an important role. One of his most critical beliefs was in social Darwinism—the idea that within society or politics, constant struggle would lead the fittest to survive. Thus, Hitler encouraged his subordinates to use their initiative and carve out their own power bases. If they were the "strongest and fittest" they would succeed. In a speech in 1928 at Kulmbach, Hitler told the audience that the "idea of struggle is as old as life itself." He went on to say: "In this struggle the stronger, the more able, win while the less able, the weak, lose."

On a personal level, Hitler was a vegetarian and neither smoked nor drank alcohol; he only seems to have had one personal relationship that involved any real emotional attachment. This was with his niece, Geli Raubal, who came to live with "Uncle Alf" in 1929. In 1931 she was found, aged 23, shot dead with Hitler's pistol. Hitler was obsessively jealous and carefully controlled Geli's movements and who she saw. She was chaperoned wherever she went and was effectively a prisoner.

In the final days of the Third Reich, Hitler married Eva Braun, who had been his close female companion for many years. But she was an intellectually slight woman whose role in Hitler's life was as a pretty blond companion who would not disagree with the mighty Führer.

Geli Raubal, Hitler's niece, and perhaps his only real love. She was found dead, probably having committed suicide, in 1931.

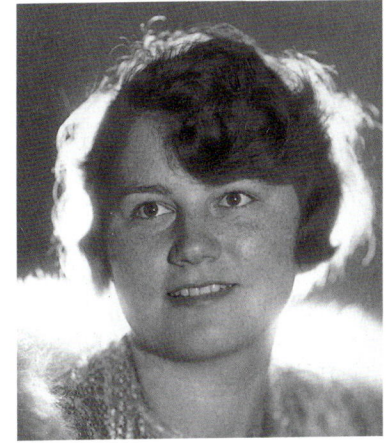

CHAPTER 2
HITLER'S RISE TO POWER

Resentful of the peace treaties of 1919 and split by political extremism, postwar Germany provided an ideal stage for a charismatic politician to rise to power on a platform of nationalism, militarism, and intolerance. Manipulating democratic politics to get into power, Hitler then ruthlessly created a dictatorship and began planning wars of conquest.

World War II Begins

Previous pages: German sailors and soldiers during the attempted revolution in 1919.

In October 1918, a key Allied condition for peace negotiations was that Kaiser Wilhelm should abdicate. He did so on November 9, ending the monarchy in Germany. The country was proclaimed a republic, and two days later the civilian government signed the armistice ending World War I. But by that point, Germany was already very unstable. Instability and weak government bedevilled the country for over a decade, until Hitler came to power in 1933.

At the start of November 1918, a naval mutiny turned into a widespread revolt. Workers set up councils in many cities. Political violence erupted on the streets. In December 1918, the extreme left formed the German Communist Party (KPD). The following month the German Workers' Party (DAP) was set up on the extreme right. It was this party—later the National Socialist German Workers' Party (NSDAP), or the Nazis—that World War I veteran Adolf Hitler joined in September 1919.

The Weimar Republic

In January 1919, the communist Spartacus League staged a coup in the capital, Berlin. Four months later, the state of Bavaria declared itself a soviet republic. Both risings were put down by right-wing paramilitaries sent in by the government. Known as *Freikorps*, these groups of ex-servicemen proved hard to control.

Against this background, an assembly met to draw up a new constitution. Because Berlin was unsafe, it met in the city of Weimar. Historians refer to the government it created as the Weimar Republic. Its early years were marked by short-lived coalitions. While elections took place, uprisings continued. In March 1920, a right-wing coup failed to take power in Berlin. Political killings were also common during this period. In June 1922, for example, anti-Semitic nationalists killed Germany's Jewish foreign minister, Walther Rathenau.

A Workers' Defense Force militia unit deployed for action, somewhere in Germany in 1921.

First appearance of the Nazis

In 1920, the NSDAP issued its political platform, which included the rejection of the Versailles Treaty, German territorial expansion, and the disbarment of Jews from citizenship. The following year Hitler became chairman and organized the party's private army, the *Sturmabteilung* (SA). Labeled the Brownshirts, the SA roamed the streets fighting with opponents.

Over the next few years, the fledgling Weimar Republic struggled against pressures both within and outside Germany. A major problem it faced was the fact that it accepted that Germany had caused World War I, and that the Allied powers had the right to be paid reparations by Germany. However, the perception of many in Germany was that Versailles was unfair. It was, in their eyes, a punitive "Carthaginian Peace" designed to crush German strength forever. There were those in Britain, such as the economist John Maynard Keynes, who supported this view in books such as *The Economic Consequences of the Peace* (1919). For a population trying to come to terms with defeat and economic depression, the idea of a punitive peace soon took hold. Many in Germany even questioned whether they had been defeated at all. After all, Germany was not occupied when the war ended in November 1918, and the German Army had withdrawn from the front in France and Belgium at the war's end in good order. This was the "Stab-in-the-Back" myth that proved very powerful in all sections of German society: the idea that it was

Hitler using his considerable speech-making skills at a meeting in Germany in the interwar years.

> "A naval mutiny turned into a widespread revolt"

BENITO MUSSOLINI

Mussolini's rise to power in Italy preceded Hitler's in Germany by 11 years, and in the 1920s Mussolini was Europe's leading fascist dictator. He began his career as a socialist, but in World War I saw that the nationalist right offered a surer route to power. In 1921 he was elected to parliament, with 34 other fascist deputies. He moved to consolidate fascism by founding the National Fascist Party (PNF). Coming to power in October 1922, he manipulated the 1924 elections to seize absolute power. Mussolini gave himself the title of Il Duce (the leader) in 1925. For five years, Mussolini oversaw a social and economic revolution intended to make the state and its leader the focus of the nation's efforts. From the mid-1930s, he boosted his popularity by a series of foreign wars. Intervention in the Spanish Civil War in 1936, however, drew the regime into alliance with Germany, which led to Italy's disastrous entry into World War II. In July 1943 Mussolini was overthrown. He survived with Hitler's help until April 1945, when he was captured and executed by communist partisans.

World War II Begins

Hitler addresses a Nazi Party rally in the palace park at Tiefurt. These early events were a foretaste of the well-planned rallies that were held after the Nazis came to power in 1933.

Marxists and Jews on the home front who had betrayed the army.

Germany was forced to forfeit all of its overseas empire by the Versailles Treaty, and had lost significant amounts of territory in Europe. A major part of the western Germany, the Rhineland, was placed under international control, while a considerable part of new Germany, East Prussia, was separated from the rest of the country by land allocated to the newly reconstituted nation of Poland.

The reparations themselves were fixed at $26 billion, a huge sum. When the German Government was unable to pay in 1923, French troops occupied parts of the Ruhr, one of Germany's main industrial areas.

Soon, Germany was in the grip of a growing economic crisis. It suffered a catastrophic inflationary spiral. A loaf of bread that cost half a mark (Germany's currency) in December 1918 cost 163 marks by December 1922, 1,465 marks by June 1923, and 201 billion marks that November. This hyperinflation wiped out savings. It made many people bitter at the government's inability to solve the problem, and further undermined the legitimacy of the Weimer Republic.

Hitler's move for power

Hitler moved to take advantage of the unpopularity of the government. On November 9, 1923, he led an uprising, or *putsch*, in Munich to take control of the Bavarian government. The putsch failed and Hitler was jailed. However, his trial gave him a platform to push the Nazis into the public eye.

The failure of the putsch had another important result. It convinced Hitler that violence alone would not bring him to power, and that he needed to work within the democratic system for the time being.

Mein Kampf is a mixture of autobiography and political ideas. Hitler dictated the book in prison after the failed Beer Hall Putsch of 1923. The book outlined Hitler's beliefs and political program. It clearly displayed all his prejudices. He created a racial hierarchy in which Germans were at the top and Jews at the bottom. Hitler blamed the Jews for Germany's problems. He claimed that they were intent on world domination and were trying to pollute "superior" races by marrying into them. He also ranted against communism, democratic government, and capitalism. The book outlined Hitler's projected program in the wider world, much of which later took place. He believed that Germany needed more territory and that it would acquire it by military action. The book predicted rearmament, the rejection of the Versailles Treaty, and war with France and the Soviet Union.

Berlin Jews gather in the street. The economic problems Germany experienced in the interwar period allowed the Nazis to whip up anti-Semitism as part of their racist policies and the search for scapegoats.

For the rest of the decade, Hitler concentrated on building electoral support. Meanwhile the liberal government of Gustav Stresemann ended hyperinflation by introducing a new currency, and the Weimar Republic became more stable.

Calm before the storm

Germany's economic recovery was aided by the start in autumn 1924 of the Dawes Plan. The plan rearranged Germany's reparations payments and allowed for huge U.S. loans to help pay them. The period of relative recovery continued with the signing of the Treaty of Locarno in October 1925. Germany accepted its western boundaries as laid down in the Versailles Treaty. In return, Germany was allowed to join the League of Nations the following year.

In 1929, the Young Plan (named for U.S. businessman Owen D. Young) cut reparations to around 25 percent of the 1921 demand. Hitler supported a nationalist campaign against the plan, because it still followed the terms of the hated Versailles Treaty. In December 1929, however, a large majority of Germans voted to accept the plan. It seemed that Germany had no desire for the nationalists or the NSDAP.

Events elsewhere, however, were soon to change the situation dramatically. In autumn 1929, a crisis of confidence hit the USA. It prompted U.S. investors to begin selling their stocks and shares. The selling turned into a panic, culminating in Black Tuesday, October 29. More than 16 million shares were sold, wiping billions of dollars from the worth of U.S. corporations. The United States raised tariffs, or taxes on imports, to protect

> "In autumn 1929, a crisis of confidence hit the USA"

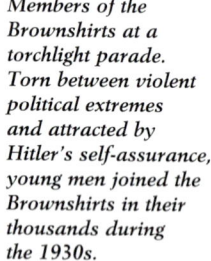

Members of the Brownshirts at a torchlight parade. Torn between violent political extremes and attracted by Hitler's self-assurance, young men joined the Brownshirts in their thousands during the 1930s.

Hitler's Rise to Power

German girls practice the Nazi salute in the town of Coburg. Women had a particular place in Nazi ideology: mainly to stay in the home and produce children.

its industry. Other nations followed suit, and the new tariffs effectively stifled international trade. The resulting global slump was a major cause of the Great Depression, a long period of great economic hardship.

Nowhere was this hardship felt more than in Germany. The country's economic well-being depended on U.S. loans that soon dried up. German companies went bankrupt, laying off millions of workers. In December 1929, unemployment in Germany stood at 1.8 million. By early 1933, it had reached more than 6 million. That was a quarter of the labor force. Over a similar period, industrial output fell by around 40 percent. Once again, ordinary Germans felt that the Weimar Republic had failed them. Many looked for an alternative to extremist parties such as Hitler's NSDAP.

Hitler's appeal

As in the early 1920s, Hitler's policies struck a chord with wide sections of the public. The middle classes, for example, had been financially hard hit for the second time in less than a decade. Even moderate Germans resented the Treaty of Versailles. Hitler appealed to them with his promise to restore Germany to its correct position in the world. At the same time he blamed Germany's problems on an alliance of Jews,

THE GREAT DEPRESSION

Extremism in Europe was intensified by the hardship that resulted from the Great Depression of the 1930s. The financial crash that struck Wall Street in October 1929 was disastrous for European nations reliant on U.S. trade and loans. Germany soon felt the effects as the United States called in its loans and cut back its imports. By 1932 German industrial production had fallen by 46 percent. People whose lives were ruined by the economic collapse began to look to the far right for answers. Elsewhere, too, people saw democratic politics as a cause of the crisis. Dictators took power in smaller countries, such as António Salazar in Portugal and Ioannis Metaxas in Greece, by promising to control the economic chaos in their countries. The crisis seemed to vindicate Mussolini's fascists in Italy, who in the mid-1920s had brought the economy largely under government control. Some observers saw Italy's success in avoiding the worst of the Depression as proof that fascism worked. Austria, for example, reorganized its industry in a similar model of state corporations.

World War II Begins

Dr. Josef Goebbels casts his vote in Berlin, 1933. The organizational abilities of Hitler's propaganda supremo gave the Nazi Party many votes in the elections of the 1920s.

communists, and bankers. The portrayal of these groups as scapegoats drew on stereotypes familiar in German culture. Hitler's powerful arguments, plus a careful use of propaganda, brought the Nazi Party rapid success. It had won only 12 seats in the 1928 election to the Reichstag (parliament). In September 1930, however, the NSDAP won 107 seats. It became the second-largest party, behind the moderate Social Democrats (SPD), who were in power.

Eyewitness Report:

" There were quite a few Storm Troopers who had Jewish girlfriends and therefore a lot of Germans just thought, 'Oh well, it's not going to be so bad—they have Jewish girlfriends, they can't hate us all.' A Nazi said to me, 'You really should be one of us.' I said, 'Look, I can't, I'm a Jew,' and he would say: 'We don't mean you, decent chaps like you will be perfectly all right in the new Germany. "

Eugene Leviné, a Jew and communist, 1933

Maneuvering for power

No party had a parliamentary majority, making the passage of new laws difficult. As in many economic crises, the ruling party, in this case the SPD, found itself unpopular in trying to control the economy in a devastating world downturn. The Weimar constitution gave considerable power to the president, who in this period was Field Marshal Paul von Hindenburg, head of the army at the end of World War I, and no friend of liberal politicians.

In April 1932, Hitler stood against Hindenburg in the presidential election and won 37 percent of the vote. Chancellor Heinrich Brüning feared that the Nazis were about to try to seize power in a coup. Three days after the presidential election, he banned the Nazis' private armies: the SA and the Schutzstaffel (SS). The SS had been formed in 1925 as protection for Hitler. Brüning's move was unpopular among conservative Germans. In late May,

Hindenburg replaced Brüning with the conservative Franz von Papen.

In return for Hitler's support, Papen lifted the ban on the Nazis' private armies. Street battles broke out between the SA and SS on the one hand and communist paramilitaries on the other. Papen called a national election for July 31, 1932. In the election, Hitler's NSDAP emerged as the largest party, with 37.3 percent of the vote and 230 seats. Hindenburg offered Hitler the post of vice chancellor. Hitler insisted upon becoming chancellor; Hindenburg refused. Papen kept the job, but in the autumn the Reichstag passed a vote of no confidence in him. Fresh elections were called for November.

A fateful misjudgment

In the November 6 election, the Nazis lost ground to the communists. They remained the largest party in the Reichstag, however, with 196 seats.

Hindenburg still would not make Hitler chancellor. Instead he appointed General Kurt von Schleicher to the post. Schleicher had no more support in parliament than Papen. His administration was over in 57 days.

In early January 1933, Papen met with Hitler. He proposed a coalition government, with Hitler as chancellor and himself as vice chancellor. Papen convinced Hindenburg that, with only three Nazis in the government, Hitler could be kept in check. Hindenburg finally agreed to make Hitler chancellor. The fatal miscalculation of Germany's conservative right was to believe that Hitler could be controlled once in power.

THE GERMAN COMMUNIST PARTY

The German Communist Party (KPD) was the largest communist party outside the Soviet Union after the end of World War I. The party was highly active, leading the Spartacist uprising of January 1919 and forming a soviet republic in Bavaria in April. In the early years of the Weimar Republic, the KPD fared better in the elections than Hitler's Nazi Party, but from 1930 onward it lost ground. Under the leadership of Ernst Thälmann, the KPD waged war on the moderate socialists of the SPD, preventing the political left uniting against Hitler. In 1933, after the Reichstag building was set on fire by a communist, Hitler outlawed the Communist Party. Under the Nazis thousands of KPD members were jailed, exiled, or killed.

Hitler with the German President Paul von Hindenburg. Germany's ruling élite hoped to control Hitler and use him to smash the forces of revolution.

Germans vacation on the Baltic coast during the 1930s. Ordinary German workers found their living conditions improved enormously under the Nazi regime.

Hitler consolidates power

Once he had become chancellor, Hitler moved swiftly to secure the Nazis' hold on power. Although there were only three Nazi politicians in the national cabinet, Hermann Göring, one of the key Nazi leaders, was minister of the interior in Prussia, which included the main German city, Berlin, a key communist stronghold. In February, Göring purged the Prussian police of any left-wing sympathizers. He then enlisted 40,000 Nazis as auxiliaries to crush any resistance to the Nazis.

Hitler called an election for March and events played into his hands perfectly. On February 27, 1933, a fire was started in the Reichstag by a communist arsonist. The new chancellor was able to suspend civil liberties and ban the German Communist Party (KPD). The episode enabled the Nazis to stir up fear of the communist threat during the election campaign. It also supported Hitler's insistence on an Enabling Act, which would make the chancellor all powerful, to protect the nation.

In the March 5 election, the NSDAP increased its number of seats to 288. It lacked an overall majority, but by alliances and intimidation, Hitler got the Enabling Act passed on March 23.

Hitler soon used his new dictatorial powers. In a bid to crush political opposition, between March and July 1933 he outlawed all parties other than the NSDAP, and also abolished trade unions. He began locking up his political opponents in SA-run concentration camps. By the end of 1933 there were about 150,000 prisoners in such camps, the most important of which was at Dachau, near Munich. Meanwhile, the

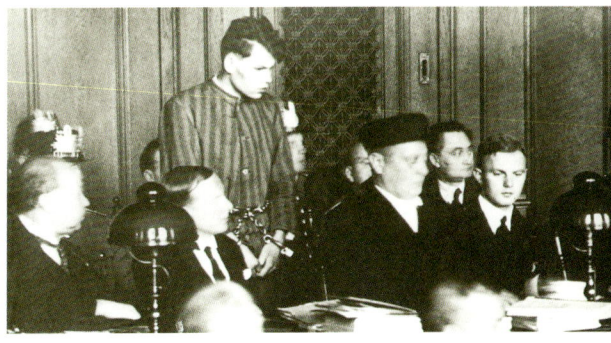

The Reichstag arsonist, a simple-minded Dutchman named Marinus van der Lubbe, stands trial for arson. He was executed, but it has never been fully established whether he was really to blame or whether he was a scapegoat.

SA men round up suspected communists during the reign of terror that began in 1933 when SA members were recruited by Göring as police auxiliaries.

Nazis extended their control over all areas of life. The Gestapo (secret police) was set up in April 1933 to monitor and arrest potential opponents of the regime. The Nazis also took over the media, closely controlling the output of the German cinema industry, closing down liberal or Jewish-owned newspapers, and allowing no voices of dissent on the national radio. Particularly noteworthy in the 1930s were the attacks on modern art and the public burning of books that the Nazis disagreed with.

Purges and murder

As the Nazis tightened their grip on Germany, however, divisions appeared in the party itself. In summer 1934, Hitler became concerned about the leftish politics of senior officers in the SA, which was now four million strong, and in particular of its leader, Ernst Röhm. He and many of his followers wanted a further radicalization of Germany, to include state control of private enterprise and SA control of the army. Röhm had powerful enemies in the army and in the Nazi Party itself, including SS chief Heinrich Himmler. Himmler and high-ranking Nazi Hermann Göring convinced Hitler that Röhm was planning a coup.

On the night of June 29–30, 1934, Nazi police and the SS rounded up Röhm and other SA officers. Many, including Röhm, were executed. Hitler also rid himself of other potential opponents, among them former chancellor Schleicher. The so-called "Night of the Long Knives," during which perhaps 1000 people died, shocked and terrified the German public. In August, following the death of Hindenburg, Hitler strengthened his own position.

> "The Night of the Long Knives shocked and terrified the German public"

Members of the SA pass a set of posters with crude Jewish stereotypes. Der Stürmer was a weekly Nazi newspaper that specialized in such images. It was said to be the only newspaper that Hitler read from cover to cover.

German students and Nazi paramilitaries burn so-called un-German books in Berlin in May 1933. A band played as 20,000 books were destroyed.

He merged the posts of president and chancellor into a single office. Hitler took the title of Führer (leader)—and with it absolute power in Germany. Further constitutional changes included changing the federal structure of Germany into one unitary state.

Religion was an area that Hitler was also determined to control. An agreement with the Pope in 1933 meant that Catholic criticism was effectively silenced, and when Protestant opposition surfaced it was swiftly dealt with. Late in 1935, 700 Protestant pastors were arrested. The following year, over 800 more were taken into custody for protesting at attacks on churches and anti-Semitism.

Anti-Semitism had been a key part of Nazi ideology since the early 1920s, and Hitler began to take action against Germany's Jews soon after taking power. The German Jewish community was 650,000 strong in 1933, and had been the victim of direct Nazi attacks since 1930. Synagogues and cemeteries had been targets for SA violence and some Jews were actually murdered. Once Hitler became chancellor, such violence escalated. Then, in April 1933, Hitler instituted a boycott of Jewish businesses. He went on to enact a series of laws against the Jewish community, including the Nuremberg Laws of 1935. This set of measures stripped Jews of their German citizenship, forbade marriage between Jews and others, and barred

Eyewitness Report:

❝ We had three elderly ladies who were living on the first floor with us. One was dragged out and beaten up for no reason except that she got in the way or something. I was knocked about and finally ended up in the cellar ... I was absolutely in shock. I couldn't understand how this situation had arisen. It was uncalled for violence against a people they didn't know. ❞

Rudi Bamber, nine years old at the time of Kristallnacht

A Nazi rally at Nuremberg in 1934. In the center of the picture are Hitler (middle), Heinrich Himmler (left, the head of the SS), and Victor Lutze (right, chief of the SA).

Jews from the professions (and most other forms of employment).

The worst single example of Nazi anti-Semitism during the period before 1939 was *Kristallnacht*, the "Night of Broken Glass." In retaliation for the murder of a German diplomat in Paris by a Polish Jew, Nazi storm troopers raided and destroyed Jewish homes and businesses in an orgy of violence. Nearly 200 synagogues were burnt down. What few rights Germany's Jews still possessed were then rescinded. By 1939, over 400,000 Jews had emigrated. Most of those that remained then died in the greater horror of the Holocaust during World War II.

An economic miracle?

While many Germans protested at Hitler's racial policies, many more did not. This was partly because the police state that had been set up made any sign of dissent very dangerous; but it was also true that many Germans did well out of the new regime. Many army officers were enthusiastic supporters of Hitler's decision to rearm; similarly, industrialists did well under Hitler, as did many of their employees.

Hitler put Hjalmar Schlact in charge of the economy soon after he came to power. Schlact put people to work by implementing a program of public works and borrowing heavily. A new motorway system of *autobahns* was built, for example. Within two years, Schlact had reduced unemployment from six million to under three million. He resigned in 1937, but a policy of sustained rearmament under Hermann Göring then kept the German economy booming. The boom could certainly not have continued for much longer than 1939, but during the mid-1930s the average German worker felt much better

SA men stick propaganda posters on a store during a boycott of Jewish businesses in 1933. The Nazis began to encourage German anti-Semitism almost as soon as they took power.

NUREMBERG RALLIES

Held for the first time in 1923, the party rally of the NSDAP settled in Nuremberg from 1927. Lasting for several days in September, the rally was a meticulously organized theatrical spectacle designed to show off the power and sense of unity of the German people and their Nazi ideology. The program included torchlit rallies, speeches by party leaders to huge audiences, and parades in front of Hitler himself. As up to 500,000 of the party faithful from all over Germany gathered to pledge their loyalty to the Führer, the rally could take on an almost religious quality. Josef Goebbels, the Nazi propaganda specialist, referred to the event as "the High Mass of our party." The Nuremberg rallies were filmed and shown in German cinemas and at party gatherings. The most famous example is Leni Riefenstahl's movie documentary of the 1934 rally, *Triumph of the Will*. The Nuremberg rallies ceased after 1938, the 1939 event being cancelled because of the outbreak of World War II.

World War II Begins

off than during the period 1930–33.

It was not just secure employment that made the German worker feel good about the Nazi regime. The unions may have been banned, but workers became members of the German Labor Front (German acronym DAF), which organized holidays with travel expenses and workers' education programs.

Strength Through Joy

The Strength Through Joy holiday movement, heavily funded by the Nazis, also offered holidays to ordinary Germans for the first time. Hundreds of thousands of Germans went on cruises on luxury liners (two of which were built specially for Strength Through Joy).

It was not only industrial workers who enjoyed prosperity under Nazi rule. The peasant farmers of Germany were given priority by the new regime, and although the results were not as successful as in heavy industry, the countryside was generally happy under Nazi rule.

Economic well being was boosted by something wider: a sense that Germany would now achieve its proper place in the world, a place that it was denied during the Weimar Republic. The great rallies of the mid-1930s, especially those held at Nuremberg, grandiose building projects under architect Albert Speer, the hosting of the Olympic Games in 1936, and Hitler's decision to ignore the Versailles Treaty and rearm the German military enthused German nationalists. They were even more encouraged by Hitler's decision to expand Germany's role on the international stage, and to overturn the Versailles Treaty entirely. They were not to know that this would lead to eventual catastrophe.

SPOTLIGHT

THE HITLER YOUTH

Hitler was determined to spread Nazi ideology among the young people of Germany. The Hitler Youth was the most important expression of this drive.

By the end of 1933, all other youth organizations (apart from some Catholic groups) had been either banned or subsumed into the Hitler Youth. By early 1934, nearly half of all boys between 10 and 14 were in the Hitler Youth, while 15 percent of girls between those ages were in its female equivalent, the Young Girls' League. This was a sustained attempt to indoctrinate the young people of Germany.

Far left: Baldur von Schirach, Reich Youth Leader. A devoted admirer of Hitler, he was appointed head of the Hitler Youth in 1933.

Above: Members of the Hitler Youth eating outdoors. In some ways, the Hitler Youth was the equivalent of the Scouting movement elsewhere.

Below left: A Hitler Youth rally in Germany in the 1930s.

Below: A Hitler Youth marching practice. Where the Hitler Youth was unlike the Boy Scout movement was in its emphasis on military skills.

Above right: A group of Hitler Youth are shown the workings of a machine gun. The organization was designed in part to act as a form of military training.

Right: More explicit military training with rifles on the firing range in the 1930s.

Below right: A map reading exercise for young Germans. In 1933, Hitler described how he wanted a new generation "swift as the greyhound, tough as leather, and hard as Krupp steel."

CHAPTER 3
EUROPE IN CRISIS: 1935–1939

As Hitler's position grew more secure within Germany, he began a campaign of territorial expansion that was initially met with inaction by France and Britain but that eventually drove the continent to war.

World War II Begins

*Previous pages:
A mass Nazi Party rally at Nuremberg in the 1930s.*

British prime minister Neville Chamberlain (center right) and German foreign minister Joachim von Ribbentrop (right) review a guard of honor at the Munich Conference in September 1938. French and British concessions at the conference failed to stop Europe's slide toward war.
▼

Adolf Hitler made no secret of his opposition to the 1919 Treaty of Versailles, which limited Germany's armed forces, and had reduced Germany in size. Many Germans shared his resentment at the treaty. They thought it was unjustifiably harsh. As early as February 1933, Hitler shared with his generals a plan to take back the Sudetenland—a German-speaking area of Czechoslovakia—and make a union with Austria, before defeating France, Poland, and Russia. Few of his listeners took him seriously. Within a few years, however, it would become clear that Hitler was deadly serious.

International relations

In October 1933, Hitler took Germany out of the permanent disarmament talks in Geneva and the League of Nations, the body set up to solve international disputes. Hitler signed a nonaggression pact with his eastern neighbor, Poland, in January 1934, removing any danger of a pre-emptive Polish strike on Germany.

Suspicion

Hitler also sought to make alliances within Europe. The most obvious ally was Italy, governed by Benito Mussolini. There were parallels between Mussolini's fascism and Hitler's Nazism, and the Italians also resented Versailles, which they felt had failed to reward their part in the Allied victory. Mussolini also rejected the League of Nations. When he invaded Abyssinia (Ethiopia) in October 1935, he ignored its protests.

The alliance between Hitler and

Mussolini started badly, however. Mussolini was not impressed by Hitler, and was suspicious of Hitler's plan to create a Greater Germany. Hitler envisaged an *Anschluss*, or union, with Austria, Italy's northern neighbor. Mussolini wanted to keep Austria independent as a buffer between Italy and Germany.

On July 25, 1934, Austrian Nazis, with Hitler's support, murdered the Austrian chancellor, Engelbert Dollfuss, a fierce opponent of the *Anschluss*, during a failed coup. Mussolini mobilized his army on the Austrian border, ready to support the government against Nazi aggression. Kurt von Schuschnigg, a pro-Italian fascist, became the new chancellor. To some observers in France and Britain, it seemed that Mussolini could be a useful block to Hitler's territorial expansionism.

The Saarland and Stresa

In January 1935, the people of the Saarland, a southwestern region that had been removed from Germany by the Versailles Treaty, voted to rejoin Germany. The result was celebrated as a victory for German nationalism.

In March 1935, Hitler announced that Germany would no longer accept the military limitations of Versailles. In fact rearmament had been going on for two years. By 1935, for example, the German army had increased from 100,000 to 300,000 men, while the air force—actually forbidden by Versailles—consisted of 18,000 personnel and hundreds of aircraft. Hitler was hoping that he could disregard Versailles with little danger of provoking other European powers into action.

The Stresa Front

In response to German rearmament, Mussolini called a conference with France and Britain at the Italian city of Stresa in April 1935. The so-called Stresa Front agreed to use force to

German troops cross the Rhine River during the reoccupation of the Rhineland on March 7, 1936. Hitler later said that waiting to see whether the Allies would call his bluff and move against him was one of the worst times of his life.

World War II Begins

Adolf Hitler and Nazi naval chief Admiral Erich Raeder inspect the new warship Scharnhorst *in October 1936. The Nazis ignored Versailles Treaty limitations on shipbuilding.*

defend the Versailles Treaty. The agreement soon fell apart, however, when Hitler offered to make non-aggression pacts with his neighbors. Meanwhile Britain and Italy were suspicious of a French alliance with the Soviet Union, France was angered by an Anglo–German naval agreement, and both France and Britain condemned Italy's invasion of Abyssinia. The invasion effectively marked the end of both the Stresa Front and the League of Nations, which proved powerless to prevent Italy's aggression.

With Germany openly rearming and its opposition fractured, Hitler made his next move. To protect France and the Low Countries, the Versailles Treaty had created a demilitarized zone in the Rhineland, German territory west and east of the Rhine River. The Rhineland's status had been confirmed by the Locarno Pact of 1925, under which the Allies evacuated their troops from the area in 1930. On the morning of March 7, 1936, however, Hitler sent 22,000 troops into the Rhineland.

Hitler's move was a gamble. He had promised his generals that he would withdraw if the French opposed him. The French did nothing, however, partly because they overestimated German strength and partly because they were waiting for support from Britain. The British, however, remained suspicious of France's alliance with the Soviet Union, and also underestimated the significance of the move.

Hitler and Mussolini

The failure of the democracies to prevent the remilitarization of the Rhineland marked a great strategic

BRITAIN AND FRANCE 1937–1939

A frequent question about the 1930s is why the French and British did not make a stronger stand against Hitler. Both had their own reasons for caution. France, on Germany's border, had a smaller population and economy than its neighbor, and would not have been able to defeat Germany alone. The French tried to make alliances with other European states, but still needed British support to win a war against Germany. For its part, Britain faced different problems. The British Empire was increasingly difficult to defend, particularly in East Asia, where Japan was growing in strength. However, a deeper reason for French and British reluctance to confront Hitler was that both countries had been traumatized by the losses of World War I, and were desperate to avoid another European conflict.

victory for Hitler and for Europe's dictatorships. In July 1936, Mussolini acknowledged Hitler's claim to treat Austria as a German state. In October, Mussolini and Hitler formed the Rome–Berlin Axis, and in November, Germany and Japan signed an Anti-Comintern Pact directed against the Soviet Union.

Meanwhile, Germany and Italy both supported Francisco Franco's Nationalists in the civil war that broke out in Spain in July 1936. The right-wing Nationalists were opposed by the Republicans, government forces, workers' militias, and brigades made up of volunteers from around the world. The war lasted three years before the Nationalist victory in March 1939.

Mussolini supplied 70,000 troops, plus tanks, artillery, and aircraft, to aid the Nationalists. Hitler sent fewer men but some 100 aircraft; the pilots used the conflict to perfect the techniques that would be vital in the Blitzkrieg tactics Germany employed in World War II.

The Rome–Berlin Axis opened the way for Hitler's next step after remilitarizing the Rhineland: the *Anschluss*. After the failed Nazi coup in Austria in 1934, Kurt von Schuschnigg had become chancellor with the support of Mussolini. Hitler made no secret of his determination to achieve the *Anschluss*, however, and the loss of Italian protection left Schuschnigg very vulnerable.

In February 1938, Hitler gave Schuschnigg an ultimatum: if he refused to include Nazis in his government,

> "The Rhineland marked a great strategic victory for Adolf Hitler"

Austrian Nazis in the town of Graz celebrate the Anschluss *with Germany in March 1938.*

THE ANTI-COMINTERN PACT

In November 1936, Germany and Japan signed an agreement known as the Anti-Comintern Pact. It agreed that each country would help the other if either were attacked by the Soviet Union. The pact took its name from the Comintern, or Communist International. That was a Soviet committee set up in Moscow to coordinate the activities of Communist parties around the world in the attempt to create a global revolution. Italy, which had signed a treaty of friendship with Germany, joined the agreement in 1937. The effect of the pact was therefore to bring together the three chief aggressor countries that would be described as the Axis powers during World War II.

Without French and British support, Czech president Eduard Benes had little choice but to give in to Hitler's demands.

German forces would invade Austria. With no backing from the Western democracies, the Austrian initially agreed, but then announced a plebiscite to be held to re-assert Austria's independence. During the confused period that followed, Arthur Seyss-Inquart, the leader of the Austrian Nazis, forced Schuschnigg to resign. At Hitler's insistence, Seyss-Inquart became chancellor. He then invited German troops into Austria.

On March 13, 1938, Hitler declared Austria a province of the German Reich, or empire. About a month later 99.7 percent of the Austrian people voted in favor of the *Anschluss*.

Czechoslovakia

The French and British had again failed to prevent German expansion. For many Britons, this policy of appeasement was a genuine attempt to resolve German grievances. They saw Hitler's aim to bring together all Germans under German government as an expression of the principle of self-determination. They believed that Hitler would cease when he had achieved his aims. The French, meanwhile, were more suspicious of Hitler but were reluctant to act without British support.

The democracies' failure to resist his demands encouraged Hitler to pursue further expansion. This time his target was the Sudetenland, a border area of Czechoslovakia that contained a large minority of Germans. Hitler used the Sudeten Germans as a pretext to claim the whole of Czechoslovakia.

In April 1938, under orders from Hitler, the leader of the Nazis in the Sudetenland, Konrad Henlein, began to demand self-government for the Sudeten Germans. The Czech government of Eduard Benes reacted with alarm; it called up its reservists and positioned troops along the German border. Hitler condemned what he called Czech provocation, and told his generals to prepare an invasion plan for October.

APPEASEMENT

Appeasement was the policy adopted by Britain, and to a lesser degree by France, toward Hitler's demands. Many British people regarded the Versailles Treaty as unfair toward Germany; they felt that some of Hitler's demands were just. By meeting his demands, they hoped to prevent him from making demands that risked another conflict. However, Hitler saw appeasement as weakness in his opponents. He followed each demand with another. After the occupation of Czechoslovakia, the policy lost much of its support in Britain and France. Leading politicians realized that they had to be prepared to go to war to stop Hitler.

Mussolini and Hitler (left) face Chamberlain (right, next to a translator) in Munich in September 1938. The Italians, Germans, British, and French decided the fate of Czechoslovakia without inviting the Czechs to the talks.

Again Britain and France chose not to resist Hitler's demands. British prime minister Neville Chamberlain had already told the French that he thought the Czechs should be prepared to give up territory. As the British and French convinced Benes to make concessions, however, so Hitler increased his demands. On September 12, he demanded self-determination for the Sudeten Germans and massed his troops on the border.

Fearing war was imminent, Chamberlain called a conference at Munich on September 30, 1938, to discuss the crisis. The talks were

NEVILLE CHAMBERLAIN

Neville Chamberlain, Britain's prime minister in the years leading up to the war, began a career in local politics in 1911. He joined the Conservative Party and was elected to Parliament in 1918. Chamberlain served as minister of health and chancellor of the exchequer before he became prime minister in 1937. In foreign policy Chamberlain followed a policy of appeasement, and has been widely criticized for underestimating Hitler's territorial ambitions. Chamberlain himself had an intense dislike of criticism, and did not welcome advisers who advocated different policies from his own. After appeasement failed he acknowledged that war was inevitable, and reluctantly took Britain into the conflict. Chamberlain died in 1940.

Sudeten Germans salute as German troops enter Friedland on October 3, 1938. Despite Czech concessions to the Sudeten Germans, Hitler pushed them to demand full self-determination.

attended by Britain, France, Italy, and Germany. The Czechs were not invited. Hitler got his way: the Czechs were told to evacuate the Sudetenland by October 10. If they did not, they would get no help from the French and British to resist German aggression. Chamberlain claimed that the agreement promised "peace for our time." Within a year, however, Europe was at war.

The Munich Agreement has become a notorious example of appeasement, a policy now widely discredited as naive and cowardly. Many historians believe that Hitler outwitted his opponents; Hitler himself came to the same conclusion. However, both Britain and France quickened their own rearmament. Hitler's assumption that they would not fight, based on what happened at Munich, would eventually lead him to overstep their patience.

After Munich

The Munich Agreement marked the beginning of the end of Czech independence. Czechoslovakia's other minorities, such as Slovakians and Ruthenians, demanded independence. With Hitler's support, Hungary seized territory in the south of the country. On March 15, 1939, Germany occupied the rest of the country. That same month Hitler forced Lithuania, on the Baltic coast, to hand the city of Memel—formerly part of the German state of Prussia—to Germany.

Hitler's renewed expansion in Czechoslovakia forced the Allies to recognize that in fact his ambitions could not be appeased. Chamberlain

STALIN AND THE EUROPEAN CRISIS

Wary of German expansion, Soviet leader Joseph Stalin was ready to use force to save Czechoslovakia in 1938. He would not intervene without support from France and Britain, however, and it was not forthcoming. The Western powers treated the Soviet Union as a threat rather than an ally, preferring to send diplomats rather than senior politicians to negotiate with Stalin. Western suspicions of the Soviet Union seemed well founded. Under Stalin, Soviet military and industrial power had grown considerably. The state had taken control of the economy, forbidding some forms of economic activity and imposing a series of Five Year Plans (the first was from 1928 to 1933) to increase industrial output. Meanwhile Stalin had consolidated his control of the state and become effectively a dictator. In the late 1930s he launched a series of purges to eliminate thousands of real and perceived opponents, including former Bolsheviks and experienced army officers. The loss of so many skilled leaders would greatly weaken the Red Army.

Italian Bersaglieri prepare to advance during the April 1939 occupation of Albania.

now warned Hitler not to interpret Britain's reluctance to fight as meaning that it would not fight. As war appeared increasingly inevitable, France and Britain made overtures to Germany and Italy, respectively, to buy time to rearm and to halt expansion, but such moves achieved little.

Eyewitness Report:

> Danzig is a German city and it wishes to return to Germany. I am not a democratic statesman; I am a realistic National Socialist. However, I held it equally necessary to point out to the government in Warsaw that, just as it desires access to the sea, Germany desires access to its province in the east. These are indeed difficult questions. Germany bears no responsibility for this. The ones to be blamed are the magicians of Versailles who either out of malice or thoughtlessness set up a hundred powder kegs.

Adolf Hitler, commenting on the Danzig situation, April 1939

The question of Poland

On April 7, 1939, Mussolini launched an invasion of Albania. The Italian dictator had expansionist ambitions of his own, and had declared an Italian empire after the invasion of Ethiopia in 1935. After World War I, Italy had expanded its territories along the Adriatic, the sea that separated it from the Balkans; now the Balkan state of Albania was a logical target.

Mussolini's territorial expansion was easily achieved. The invasion force of 100,000 troops and 400 aircraft soon overcame the Albanian Army. The Albanian king, Zog, went into exile and Mussolini offered the crown to the Italian king, Victor Emmanuel III.

Hitler, meanwhile, turned to what he termed "the Polish question." Modern Poland had been created by the peace treaties of 1919, and included two areas that between them were home to about a million Germans. The Baltic port of Danzig (Gdansk in Polish) was to be

Nazi banners decorate the main street of Danzig. Declared a Polish-administered Free City by the Versailles Treaty, Danzig was home to many Germans who embraced Hitler's promise to reclaim the city for Germany.

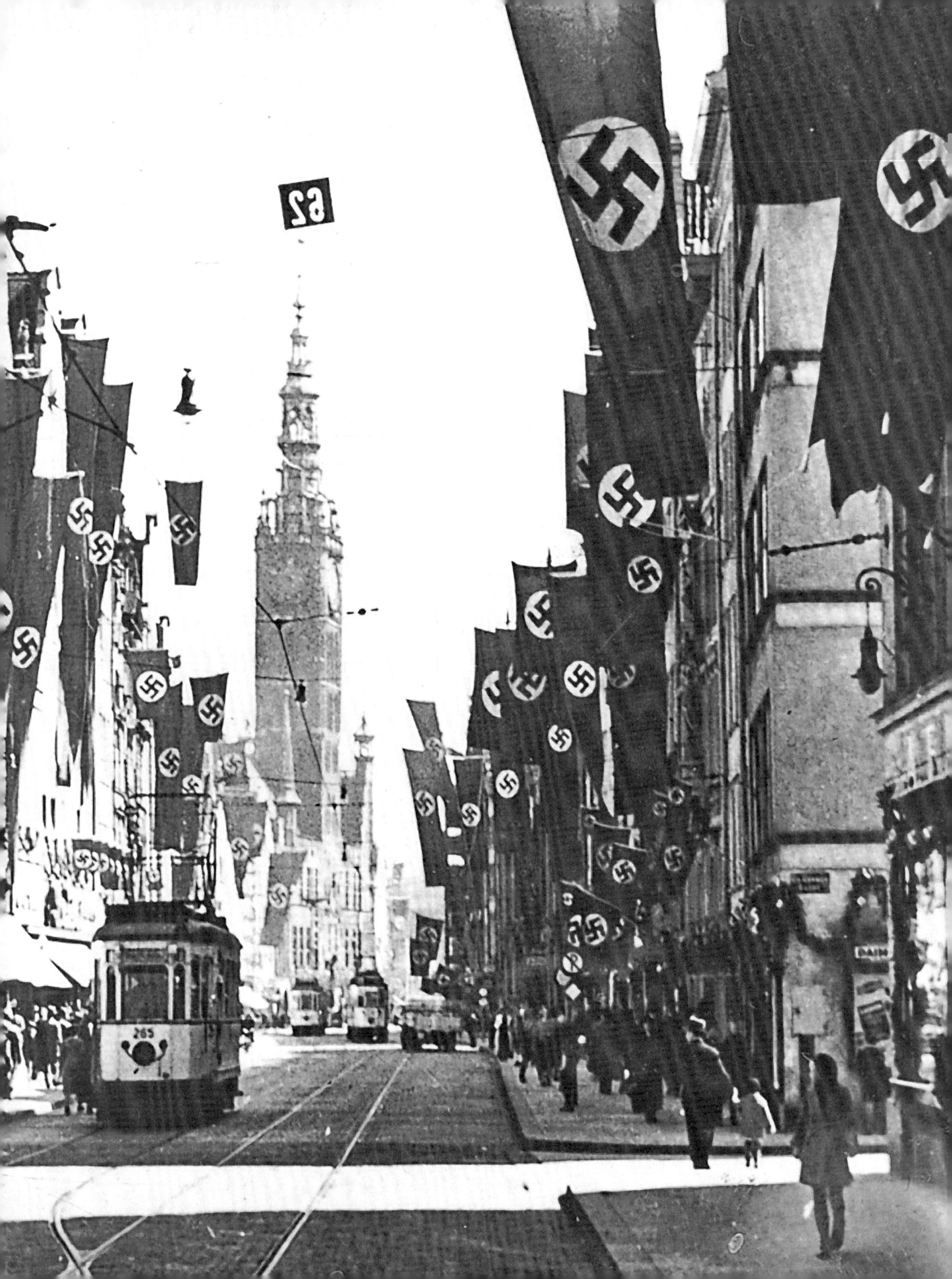

World War II Begins

Motorized German troops advance into Poland. The invasion was an early triumph for the fast-moving Blitzkrieg tactics the Germans used widely and to great effect.

> "SS troops in Polish uniforms staged a mock raid"

German troops remove a barrier at a border crossing during the invasion of Poland on September 1, 1939.

a Free City under League of Nations protection, while a narrow stretch of land known as the Polish Corridor linked Poland to Danzig and the sea, splitting Germany from its state of East Prussia.

When he had begun his expansion, Hitler largely left Poland alone, signing a nonaggression pact with it in 1934. He told the Poles that he had no designs on their territory. After the events in Czechoslovakia, however, such promises did not seem worth very much. In October 1938, Hitler proposed building a German-controlled road across the Polish Corridor and passing Danzig back to Germany. He offered to guarantee Poland's borders in return. The Poles instead signed a pact with the Soviet Union, their eastern neighbor. The Poles also made warlike noises about fighting to prevent losing territory to Germany.

Protecting Poland

Poland's determination coincided with the acceptance in the Western democracies that they had to make a stand against Nazi aggression. Britain and France offered to guarantee Polish independence. In the event of German aggression, they were committed to military action on Poland's behalf. Some historians question whether the allies were really prepared to fight in March 1939, or whether they were trying to warn Hitler off. Whatever their intentions, Hitler's chief concern lay in the east, where the Soviet Union could move troops into Poland far more easily than Britain or France.

Hitler wanted to avoid facing a possible alliance of the Soviet Union, Britain, and France. The Western democracies were equally aware of the Soviets' potential to deter German expansion, but their negotiations

Europe in Crisis: 1935–1939

with Stalin failed.

At the same time, however, Hitler had set aside his ideological differences with Stalin in the hopes of making an alliance. In August 1939 he offered Stalin a deal: if the Soviets allowed Germany to attack western Poland, they would have a free hand in eastern Poland, the Baltic states (Lithuania, Latvia, and Estonia), and Bessarabia in Romania.

Approaches to Stalin

Munich had had an important effect on Stalin, who had been prepared to go to war to protect Czechoslovakia. The capitulation of France and Britain to Hitler's demands convinced Stalin that they would be unreliable allies. He decided that he had to cope with German expansion eastward on his own, without their help. He was in continued negotiations with Britain and France during the summer of 1939, but the mutual suspicion between the Soviet dictator and the diplomats from the western democracies meant that there was no deal on the table that either side could accept.

From 1936 to August 1939, Hitler followed a policy of expansion that succeeded in creating a larger Germany without provoking war with Britain and France.

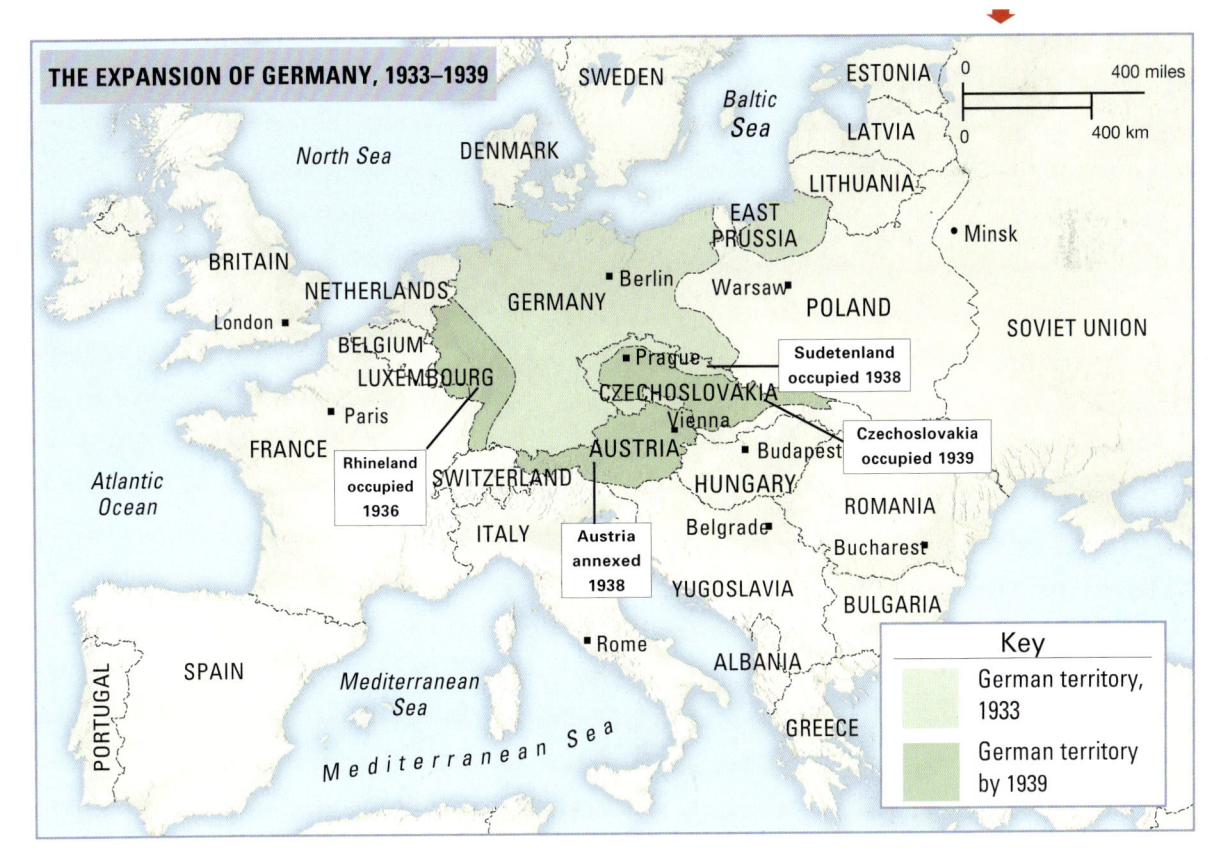

THE EXPANSION OF GERMANY, 1933–1939

- Rhineland occupied 1936
- Austria annexed 1938
- Sudetenland occupied 1938
- Czechoslovakia occupied 1939

Key:
- German territory, 1933
- German territory by 1939

45

HOME FRONT

THE OUTBREAK OF WAR

At the outbreak of war in 1914, Britain had been a jingoistic nation, confident of victory in a short campaign. In 1939, things were different. The nation realized the new conflict would be long and hard.

Most British people had been greatly relieved that war had not broken out during the Munich crisis of 1938. They had memories of the horrors of World War I, and many felt that Germany had been badly treated in the Versailles Treaty of 1919. However, Hitler's occupation of the remainder of Czechoslovakia early in 1939 made most realize that war was inevitable: that it was the only way of stopping Hitler's seemingly limitless territorial ambitions.

Below: Troops drilling on the beaches of southern England in early 1939.

Above: Enlisting in the Air Training Corps. It was clear that air power would be very important in the coming war.

Europe in Crisis: 1935–1939

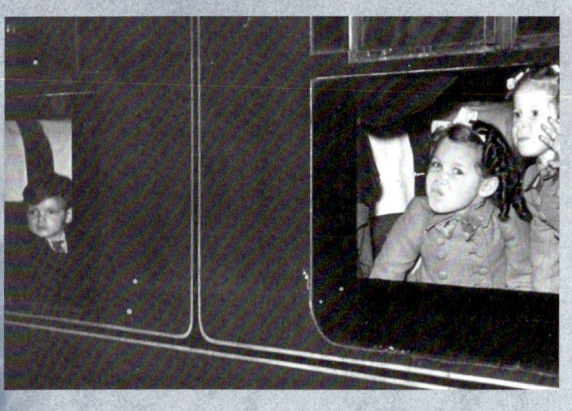

Above: Soon after the outbreak of war, the program of evacuating children from Britain's cities out into the countryside began. There was fear that cities would be destroyed by bombing.

Left: Hoardings placed around the statue of Eros in Piccadilly in April 1939, appealing for recruits. By this stage, the British people realized that war with Nazi Germany was probably inevitable.

Below: There was also fear of poison gas being dropped by aircraft. This photo was taken well before the actual outbreak of hostilities.

In late August 1939, German foreign secretary Joachim von Ribbentrop visited Moscow to sign a German–Soviet Non-aggression Pact, which included the deal over territory. The agreement between two nations at opposite political extremes—fascism on one side, communism on the other—shocked the Western world. It also left Hitler with a free hand in Poland, which was now terribly vulnerable, and meant that war was inevitable.

The war begins

Hitler now needed an excuse to invade Poland before the Poles and their allies could make more defensive preparations. On August 31, SS troops in Polish uniforms staged a mock raid on a radio station in the German border town of Gleiwitz. They left behind the bodies of 10 or so murdered concentration camp inmates in Polish uniforms.

Hitler used the apparent "Polish" raid as an excuse to invade Poland on September 1, 1939. On September 3, France and Britain declared war on Germany. World War II had begun.

The policy of appeasement that the Western democracies had undertaken from 1936 to 1938 had failed utterly. The British and French governments had completely underestimated the ambitions of Adolf Hitler, and had assumed that he would be satisfied with a rearrangement of the Versailles Treaty. They did not realize that they were effectively dealing with a madman whose aims would get bigger as he went from success to success. For much of the 1930s, they had been more fearful of international communism than of international fascism. The result was that Britain and France went to war in 1939 in an impossible attempt to defend the state of Poland, which was already doomed.

47

CHAPTER 4
BLITZKRIEG IN POLAND

When German troops began streaming across the Polish border at 04:45 hours on the morning of September 1, 1939, they set off a chain of events that engulfed the world in a war that lasted for six years.

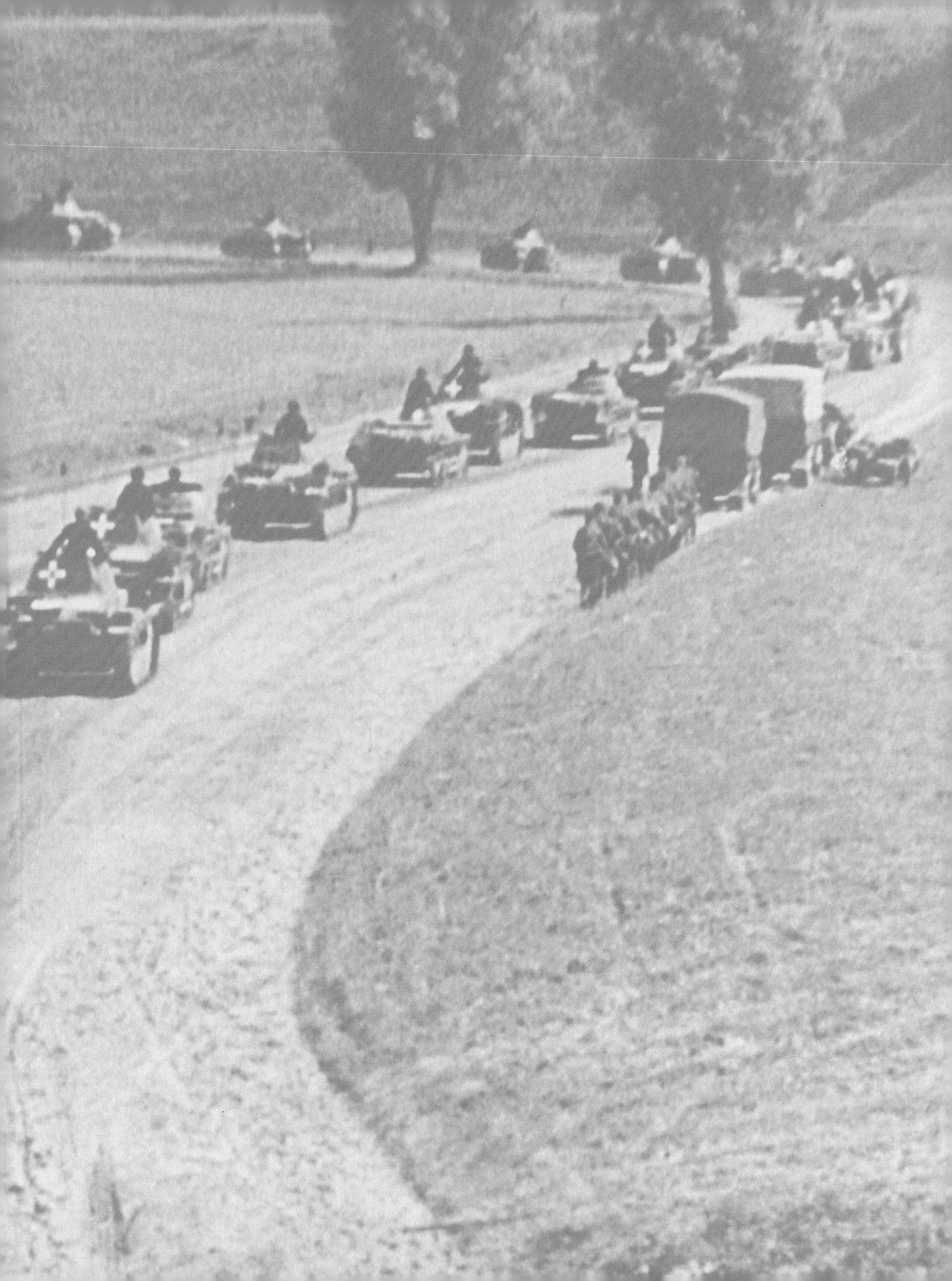

World War II Begins

Previous pages: Vehicles of a German panzer division in Poland in September 1939.

Between September 1939 and June 1940, Germany launched a series of spectacular military offensives. The first attack was against Poland and was codenamed Operation White. The German invasion force deployed two army groups made up of 55 divisions, each containing about 15,000 men. Army Group North invaded southward from East Prussia and eastward from Pomerania. The larger Army Group South attacked eastward from Silesia and Germany's ally, Slovakia. The German Air Force, or Luftwaffe, deployed over 1,800 aircraft.

> "The Luftwaffe took control of the skies within a few days"

Polish forces

Facing the German forces were 30 Polish divisions of about 12,000 troops each. Not all of them were mobilized on September 1. Those that were mobilized were positioned along Poland's borders, rather than on natural defenses such as the wide rivers within the country, in order to protect Poland's important industrial centers. The Polish forces were very exposed, as some parts of Poland were surrounded on three sides by German territory. The Polish air force had 1,900 aircraft, but of these 650 were trainers and 700 were outdated. Most would be destroyed on the ground on the first day of the war.

On September 1, 1939, the Germans began air, land, and sea attacks against Polish positions. Special forces teams were put ahead of the attack troops to sabotage telephone wires, blow up bridges, and spread confusion. During the first few days of the offensive the German forces inflicted heavy casualties on Polish frontline units and disrupted enemy supply and communications networks such as roads and railroads.

Germany advances

The Luftwaffe took control of the skies within a few days. German Stuka divebombers roamed deep behind Polish lines, machine-gunning and bombing columns of reserve troops heading for the front. German panzer divisions were sent into action against weak spots in the Polish line. Instead of fighting against the main defensive positions, they pushed behind enemy lines, aiming to capture key bridges over Poland's rivers. In the confusion, hundreds of thousands of refugees fled their homes, clogging up roads and making it difficult for the Polish to build up organized resistance.

The German and Polish infantry divisions fought dogged battles over the industrial regions of Krakow and Lodz. The lack of Polish motor transportation had an impact on the campaign, as the Poles could not retreat faster than the Germans were advancing. As the panzer divisions defeated them and pushed deeper inside Polish territory, the Poles

LIGHTNING WAR

During World War I (1914–1918) there were long periods of stalemate (deadlock), as soldiers took cover in lines of trenches. If they tried to leave the trenches to attack the enemy, they were shot down by enemy machine guns. During the 1930s German and British officers realized that using tanks offered a more effective way of waging war. Tanks had been invented during World War I, but by the 1930s had become much faster and more reliable. German officers, notably Heinz Guderian, believed that tanks could do more than break through a first line of defense. With their own support and supplies, tanks could penetrate deep into enemy territory, ruining enemy command and control, and ensuring final victory. From this theory developed the idea that breaking through frontline defenses and creating confusion behind the enemy lines could be achieved in other ways, not just with tanks. Airborne troops, such as a paratroopers, could be deployed. This method of waging war by concentrating on the attack was known in German as Blitzkrieg, or "Lightning War" in English. Against the other European armies, German Blitzkrieg tactics were highly successful and allowed Hitler to dominate the continent.

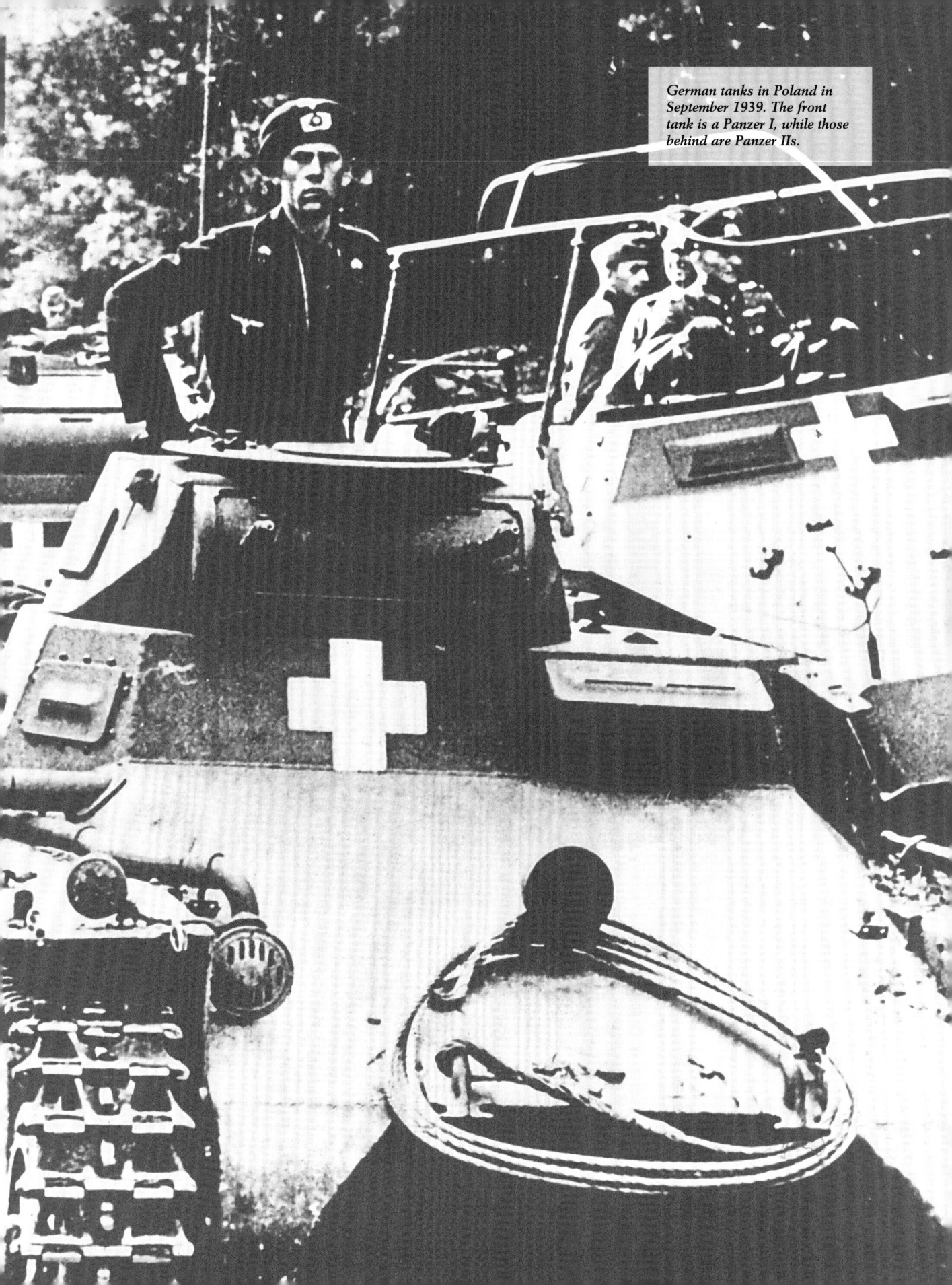

German tanks in Poland in September 1939. The front tank is a Panzer I, while those behind are Panzer IIs.

World War II Begins

Eyewitness Report:

> Very soon after that, menacing, dark bombers appeared in the blue sky over Chelm. My wife and I left the store and ran to the fields to hide. We wanted to hide in the tall wheat, but the wheat had just been harvested and we were exposed. We were terrified. German planes kept firing down at us with their machine guns, and they seemed to shriek like wild animals as they dived with their bombs and bullets. We decided to run home, and we made our way through the streets filled with panic-stricken people who were shrieking hysterically. When we arrived home, we found the old woman we had hired under the bed, holding our infant girl, Pesha, in her arms. She was so petrified that she was speechless. When the bombing ceased we went out on the street.
>
> **Kalmen Wewryk, Chelm, Poland, 1939**

A German horse-drawn supply column crosses a river during the invasion of Poland.

were left open to encirclement. After six days the Polish High Command ordered a withdrawal to the east but by then it was too late. The huge Polish armies from Posnan and Lodz were trapped around Kutno, to the west of Warsaw. The port of Danzig was quickly surrounded and cut off. German troops driving south from East Prussia had almost linked up with panzers moving up from the south, trapping Polish troops around Modlin as they did so. Only in the south was Polish resistance holding. A determined force was driving off German troops attempting to cut off the Poles' route to Romania. Romania was a potential ally and a possible entry point for Allied aid.

The trapped Polish troops at Kutno tried to make a dramatic breakout across the Bzura River to freedom. For two days the Polish kept attacking, only to be beaten back by German firepower, and by Luftwaffe attacks. The trapped troops resisted for three more weeks, when 170,000 Poles eventually emerged from the woods around Kutno to surrender.

By the second week of September, Warsaw was surrounded by German

Blitzkrieg in Poland

German troops remove a border marker on the Polish frontier in 1939, as Poland becomes part of the German Reich.

forces advancing from north, west, and south. It held out for another two weeks as, day and night, German bombers pounded the city.

Beaten back by the Germans, Polish forces were now attacked from the East. On September 17, the Soviet dictator Joseph Stalin ordered his Red Army to cross into eastern Poland. He claimed that he wanted to prevent "anarchy" caused by the collapse of the Polish government. In fact, Germany and the Soviet Union had secretly agreed to divide up Poland between them in the German–Soviet Nonaggression Pact signed in the previous month. Thousands of Soviet troops poured across the border and raced west to link up with German troops advancing east.

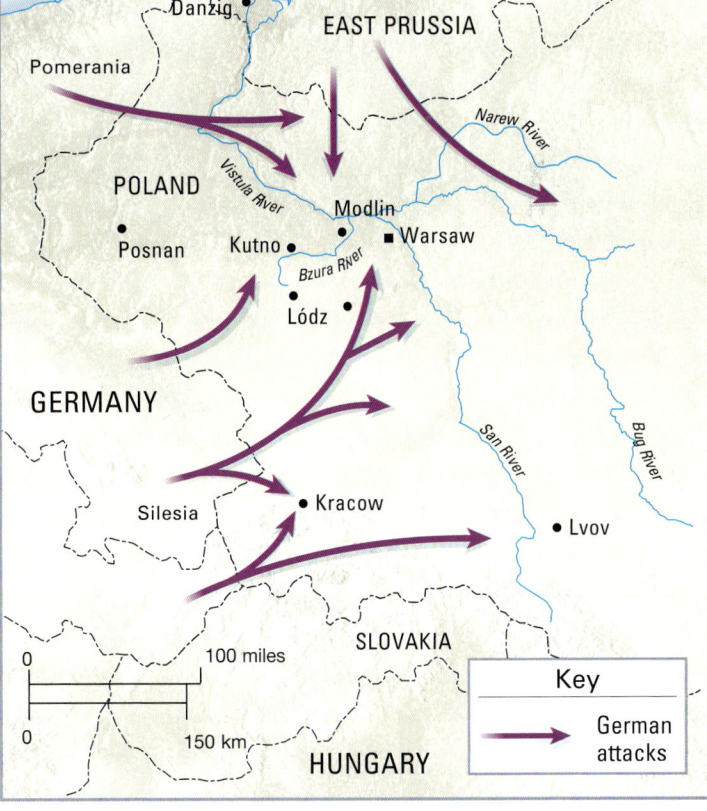

THE GERMAN INVASION OF POLAND, 1939

Key: German attacks

HOME FRONT

FIRST WEEKS OF WAR

As war broke out, the British people had to get used to a new way of life, in which many things had changed utterly.

War meant that the British people had to accept many intrusions on their privacy, and were unable to behave as they had done in the past. In particular, food was rationed. Everything anyone did had to be for the good of the country.

Left: The ration card of King George VI. The ruler of the country was happy to undergo many of the same restrictions as his subjects.

Right: Iron railings in Hyde Park, London, being torn up to be sent away to be melted down into war material.

Right above: A ration card is checked at a grocer's store. Rationing was often irritating, and a flourishing black market in certain goods soon grew up.

Center right: Crockery received by the Woman's Voluntary Service for use in the war effort.

Below right: Another important aspect of wartime life was the blackout, which also affected motorists.

Below: Digging for victory? Members of a family at work on their allotment.

Blitzkrieg in Poland

Poland collapses

Organized Polish resistance to the invaders collapsed. In the last week of September Polish troops in Modlin and Warsaw surrendered to the Germans. A small garrison of 4,500 men held out on the Hel Peninsula near Danzig until October 2. Some 694,000 Polish troops were rounded up by the victorious Germans, and more than 217,000 Poles were seized by the Red Army.

Both the Germans and Soviets treated the Poles with great brutality. Stalin ordered most of his prisoners deported to the gulag (a system of brutal labor camps) and later had thousands of Poles executed in secret at Katyn Wood in Russia.

Some 100,000 Poles managed to escape into Romania, from where they made their way to Britain and France. A Polish government-in-exile was set up in London, and many Poles joined the British armed forces. The Germans and Soviets divided up Poland, absorbing it between their countries. A new government was set up around Warsaw and run by Nazi party chiefs. They ordered the executions of Jews, intellectuals, and anyone who might rally resistance to German rule. As far as Hitler and Stalin were concerned, Poland had ceased to exist.

55

TIMELINE
SEPTEMBER 1, 1939 – SEPTEMBER 2, 1945

SEPTEMBER 1
POLAND
A German force of 53 divisions, supported by 1,600 aircraft, crosses the German and Slovakian borders into Poland in a pincer movement. World War II has begun.

SEPTEMBER 3
BRITAIN AND FRANCE
Britain and France declare war on Nazi Germany after the Nazis ignore their demands to withdraw immediately from Poland.

SEPTEMBER 9
POLAND
A Polish counterattack is launched over the Bzura River against Germany's Eighth Army. It only achieves short-term success. The Polish Army is rapidly falling to pieces under the relentless German attacks.

SEPTEMBER 17–30
POLAND
In accordance with a secret pact with Germany, the Soviet Red Army invades Poland. Little resistance is encountered on Poland's eastern border as the Polish Army is fighting for its life to the west.

SEPTEMBER 18–30
POLAND
Poland is defeated and split into two zones of occupation divided by the Bug River. Germany has lost 10,572 troops and the Soviet Union has 734 men killed in the campaign. Around 50,000 Poles are killed and 750,000 captured.

SEPTEMBER 29
SOVIET UNION
After occupying Poland, the Soviet Union concentrates on extending its control over the Baltic Sea region. During the next few weeks it gains bases and signs "mutual assistance" agreements with Lithuania, Latvia, and Estonia. Finland, however, will not agree to the Soviet Union's demands and prepares to fight.

OCTOBER 14
SEA WAR, NORTH SEA
The British battleship *Royal Oak* is sunk, with 786 lives lost, after *U-47* passes through antisubmarine defenses at Scapa Flow in the Orkneys.

NOVEMBER 30
EASTERN FRONT, FINLAND
A Soviet army of over 600,000 men, backed by air and naval power, attacks Finland. Highly-motivated Finnish troops use their familiarity with the terrain and their ability to ski through snow-covered areas to launch hit-and-run raids on Red Army units bogged down in the snow.

DECEMBER 16
FINLAND
The Red Army begins a major new offensive. To compensate for their lack of armor and artillery, the Finns use improvised explosive devices ("Molotov Cocktails," named for the Soviet foreign minister) to destroy enemy tanks.

DECEMBER 13
ATLANTIC OCEAN
British ships fight the German pocket battleship *Graf Spee* at the Battle of the River Plate. The *Graf Spee* is scuttled by its crew on December 17.

1940

MARCH 11
FINLAND
The Treaty of Moscow between Finland and the Soviet Union is agreed, ending the Winter War. Finland retains its independence but has to surrender the Karelian Isthmus and Hangö: 10 percent of its territory. Campaign losses: 200,000 Soviet troops and 25,000 Finns.

APRIL 9
NORWAY/DENMARK
A German invasion force, including surface ships, U-boats, and 1,000 aircraft, attacks Denmark and Norway. Denmark is overrun immediately.

APRIL 14–19
NORWAY
An Allied expeditionary force of over 10,000 British, French, and Polish troops lands in Norway.

MAY 7–10
BRITAIN
Prime Minister Neville Chamberlain is severely criticized over the Norwegian campaign. He resigns and is replaced by Winston Churchill.

MAY 10
THE LOW COUNTRIES
German forces invade the Low Countries. But the main German attack will take place in the south, in the Ardennes region of France.

MAY 12–14
FRANCE
German forces reach the Meuse River and fight their way across at Sedan and Dinant on May 13. German armor advances rapidly westward, opening a 50-mile (75-km) gap in the Allied line. Allied units retreat to the Channel port of Dunkirk.

MAY 26
FRANCE/BELGIUM
Operation Dynamo, the evacuation of Allied forces from the Dunkirk area, begins using small boats and naval vessels.

MAY 31
UNITED STATES
President Franklin D. Roosevelt launches a "billion-dollar defense program" to bolster the armed forces.

JUNE 1–9
NORWAY
After Britain and France reveal to the Norwegians that they are to begin an evacuation, troops begin to withdraw. King Haakon orders his Norwegians to stop fighting on June 9.

56

SEPTEMBER 1, 1939 – SEPTEMBER 2, 1945

June 3-4
FRANCE
Operation Dynamo ends. The remarkable operation has rescued 338,226 men—two-thirds of them British—from the Dunkirk beaches.

June 16-24
FRANCE
Marshal Henri-Philippe Pétain, the new French president, requests an armistice on June 17. It is agreed on the 22nd. Germany occupies two-thirds of France, including the Channel and Atlantic coastlines.

July 1
ATLANTIC OCEAN
The "Happy Time" begins for U-boat crews as their range is increased now that they have bases in French ports. This lasts until October. U-boat crews inflict serious losses on Allied convoys.

July 10
BRITAIN
The Battle of Britain begins. Hermann Göring, the Nazi air force chief, orders attacks on shipping and ports in the English Channel.

July 21
SOVIET UNION
The Soviets annex Lithuania, Latvia, and Estonia.

August 24-25
BRITAIN
The Luftwaffe inflicts serious losses on the Royal Air Force (RAF) during attacks on its main air bases in southeast England, straining the resources of Fighter Command to breaking point in a few days.

August 26-29
GERMANY
The RAF launches a night raid with 81 aircraft on Berlin following a similar raid on London. Hitler is outraged and vows revenge. German aircraft are redirected to make retaliatory raids on London. This relieves the pressure on Fighter Command's air bases.

September 7-30
AIR WAR, BRITAIN
Full-scale bombing raids on London—the "Blitz"—begin with 500 bombers and 600 fighters.

October 28
GREECE
Italy attacks Greece from Albania. The winter weather limits air support and thousands die of cold.

November 5
UNITED STATES
President Franklin D. Roosevelt is elected for a third term.

November 11-12
MEDITERRANEAN
At the Battle of Taranto, British torpedo aircraft from the carrier *Illustrious* destroy three Italian battleships and damage two other vessels during a raid on the Italian base.

December 9-11
EGYPT
The British launch their first offensive in the Western Desert. The Western Desert Force (31,000) attacks the fortified camps that have been established by the Italians in Egypt. Some 34,000 Italians are taken prisoner as they retreat rapidly from Egypt.

1941

January 2
POLITICS, UNITED STATES
President Franklin D. Roosevelt announces a program to produce 200 freighters—"Liberty" ships—to support the Allied Atlantic convoys.

February 14
NORTH AFRICA
To aid the faltering Italians, the first units of General Erwin Rommel's Afrika Korps land at Tripoli.

March 11
UNITED STATES
President Franklin D. Roosevelt signs the Lend–Lease Act that allows Britain to obtain supplies without having to immediately pay for them in cash.

April 6-15
YUGOSLAVIA/GREECE
Thirty-three German divisions, with Italian and Hungarian support, invade Yugoslavia from the north, east, and southeast. German forces also attack Greece from the north.

April 17
YUGOSLAVIA
Yugoslavia surrenders to Germany. Immediately, guerrilla forces emerge to resist the Nazi occupation.

April 27
GREECE
German forces occupy Athens. Campaign dead: Greek 15,700; Italian 13,755; German 1,518; and British 900.

May 20-22
CRETE
A German force of 23,000 men, supported by 600 aircraft, attacks Crete. The Germans launch the first major airborne operation in history.

May 23-27
ATLANTIC OCEAN
British ships find the German battleship *Bismarck* and cruiser *Prinz Eugen* in the Denmark Straits between Iceland and Greenland. The *Bismarck* sinks the cruiser *Hood* and damages the battleship *Prince of Wales*, but is then sunk.

May 28-31
CRETE
Crete falls to the Germans. British losses are 1,742 men, plus 2,011 dead and wounded at sea, while Germany has 3,985 men killed.

June 22
SOVIET UNION
Germany launches Operation Barbarossa, the invasion of the Soviet Union, with three million men divided into three army groups along a 2,000-mile (3,200-km) front. Army Group North strikes toward the Baltic and Leningrad. Army Group Center aims to take Smolensk and then Moscow. Army Group South advances toward the Ukraine and the Caucasus.

July 31
GERMANY
Reinhard Heydrich, Germany's security chief and head of the SS secret police, receives orders to begin creating a draft plan for the murder of the Jews, which becomes known as the "Final Solution."

September 30
SOVIET UNION
Operation Typhoon, the German attack on Moscow, officially begins.

TIMELINE

NOVEMBER 26
PACIFIC OCEAN
The Japanese First Air Fleet leaves the Kurile Islands on a mission to destroy the U.S. Pacific Fleet at Pearl Harbor, Hawaii.

DECEMBER 7
HAWAII
The Japanese attack Pearl Harbor. More than 183 Japanese aircraft destroy 6 battleships and 188 aircraft, damage or sink 10 other vessels, and kill 2,000 servicemen. The Japanese lose 29 aircraft.

DECEMBER 8
SOVIET UNION
Adolf Hitler reluctantly agrees to suspend the advance on Moscow for the duration of the winter.

DECEMBER 11
AXIS
Germany and Italy declare war on the United States.

1942

JANUARY 10–11
DUTCH EAST INDIES
A Japanese force begins attacking the Dutch East Indies to secure the oil assets of this island chain.

JANUARY 20
GERMANY
At the Wannsee Conference, Berlin, deputy head of the SS Reinhard Heydrich reveals his plans for the "Final Solution" to the so-called Jewish problem. Heydrich receives permission to begin deporting all Jews in German-controlled areas to Eastern Europe to face either forced labor or extermination.

FEBRUARY 8–14
SINGAPORE
Japanese troops capture Singapore. Japan has fewer than 10,000 casualties in Malaya. British forces have lost 138,000 men.

APRIL 9
PHILIPPINES
Major General Jonathan Wainright, commanding the U.S. and Filipino forces, surrenders to the Japanese.

APRIL 18
JAPAN
Lieutenant Colonel James Doolittle leads 16 B-25 bombers, launched from the carrier *Hornet*, against targets in Japan, including Tokyo.

JUNE 4
PACIFIC OCEAN
The Battle of Midway begins. Japan's Admiral Chuichi Nagumo aims to seize the U.S. base at Midway and then destroy the U.S. Pacific Fleet. Japan deploys 165 vessels, including eight carriers. The U.S. Navy has a smaller force but has three carriers. The loss of half of its carrier strength in the battle, plus 275 aircraft, puts Japan on the defensive in the Pacific.

JUNE 21
LIBYA
Following the Allied withdrawal into Egypt, the Tobruk garrison falls following German land and air attacks.

JUNE 28
SOVIET UNION
Germany launches its summer offensive, Operation Blue, with its Army Group South attacking east from Kursk toward Voronezh.

JULY 4–10
SOVIET UNION
The siege of Sevastopol ends with the Germans capturing 90,000 men.

AUGUST 7–21
GUADALCANAL
The U.S. 1st Marine Division lands on Guadalcanal Island to overwhelm the Japanese garrison.

SEPTEMBER 2
POLAND
The Nazis are "clearing" the Jewish Warsaw Ghetto. Over 50,000 Jews have been killed by poison gas or sent to concentration camps.

OCTOBER 23
EGYPT
The Battle of El Alamein begins. Some 195,000 Allied troops launch an attack against 104,000 Axis men.

NOVEMBER 2–24
EGYPT/LIBYA
Rommel, severely lacking supplies, decides to withdraw from El Alamein. Germany and Italy have lost 59,000 men killed, wounded, or captured. The Allies have suffered 13,000 killed, wounded, or missing.

NOVEMBER 19
SOVIET UNION
General Zhukov launches a Soviet counteroffensive at Stalingrad to trap the Germans in a massive pincer movement.

1943

FEBRUARY 2
SOVIET UNION
The siege of Stalingrad ends. Field Marshal Friedrich Paulus and 93,000 German troops surrender.

FEBRUARY 14–22
TUNISIA
In the Battle of the Kasserine Pass, Rommel's forces cause panic among U.S. troops. He loses 2,000 men; the Americans 10,000.

APRIL 17
GERMANY
The U.S. Eighth Army Air Force attacks Bremen's aircraft factories from its bases in eastern England. Sixteen of the 115 B-17 Flying Fortress bombers from the raid are lost.

MAY 13
TUNISIA
Axis forces surrender. Some 620,000 casualties and prisoners have been sustained by Germany and Italy. Allied campaign losses: French 20,000; British 19,000; and U.S. 18,500.

JULY 5
SOVIET UNION
More than 6,000 German and Soviet tanks and assault guns take part in the Battle of Kursk.

JULY 9
SICILY
U.S. and British troops begin an attack on Sicily.

JULY 12–13
SOVIET UNION
At Kursk, the Soviets launch a counter-offensive around Prokhorovka and an enormous tank battle develops. The German offensive is defeated.

SEPTEMBER 1, 1939 – SEPTEMBER 2, 1945

August 11–17
SICILY
The Germans finally start withdrawing before U.S. forces enter Messina on the 17th.

September 9
ITALY
Lieutenant General Mark Clark's U.S. Fifth Army, plus the British X Corps, lands in the Gulf of Salerno.

September 25
SOVIET UNION
The Soviets recapture Smolensk in their continuing offensive. Germany's Army Group Center is now falling back in some disarray.

November 6
SOVIET UNION
The Soviets recapture Kiev.

December 26
ARCTIC OCEAN
At the Battle of the North Cape, the German battleship *Scharnhorst* is sunk.

1944

January 14–27
SOVIET UNION
The Red Army ends the German blockade of Leningrad. Some 830,000 civilians have died during the siege.

January 22
ITALY
Troops of the Allied VI Corps make an amphibious landing at Anzio, behind the German lines.

March 7–8
BURMA/INDIA
Operation U-Go, the Japanese offensive to drive the Allies back into India by destroying their bases at Imphal and Kohima, begins.

March 20–22
ITALY
Despite further frontal attacks by New Zealand troops, German defenders repulse all efforts to dislodge them from Monte Cassino.

May 18
ITALY
The Allies capture the monastery of Monte Cassino.

June 6
FRANCE
The Allies launch the greatest amphibious operation in military history: D-Day. Some 50,000 men land on five invasion beaches to establish a toehold in Normandy. Allied casualties are 2,500 dead.

June 19–21
PHILIPPINE SEA
Battle of the Philippine Sea. Japan's Combined Fleet is defeated by the U.S. Fifth Fleet. The Japanese lose 346 aircraft and two carriers. U.S. losses are 30 aircraft and have one battleship slightly damaged.

June 22
SOVIET UNION
The Red Army launches Operation Bagration against Germany's Army Group Center.

July 20
GERMANY
An attempt is made by German officers to assassinate Adolf Hitler. It fails to kill the Führer.

August 1
POLAND
The Warsaw Uprising begins. Some 38,000 soldiers of the Polish Home Army battle with about the same number of German troops.

August 25
FRANCE
The commander of the German garrison of Paris, General Dietrich von Choltitz, surrenders to the Allies.

September 17
HOLLAND
Operation Market Garden, an Allied armored and airborne thrust across Holland to outflank the German defenses, begins. Paratroopers land at Arnhem, Eindhoven, and Nijmegen to capture vital bridges.

September 22–25
HOLLAND
The paratroopers fall back from Arnhem, leaving 2,500 dead behind.

October 2
POLAND
The last Poles in Warsaw surrender as the Germans crush the uprising. Polish deaths number 150,000. The Germans have lost 26,000 men.

October 20
PHILIPPINES
As the U.S. Sixth Army lands on Leyte Island, General Douglas MacArthur wades ashore and keeps a promise he made two years earlier: "I shall return."

October 23–26
PHILIPPINES
Following the U.S. landings on Leyte, the Japanese Combined Fleet is defeated at the Battle of Leyte Gulf.

December 16–22
BELGIUM
Hitler launches Operation Watch on the Rhine, his attempt to capture Antwerp. The thick fog means the Germans achieve complete surprise. But they fail to capture Bastogne.

1945

January 9
PHILIPPINES
The U.S. Sixth Army makes unopposed amphibious landings on Luzon.

January 27
POLAND
The Red Army liberates the Nazi death camp at Auschwitz.

January 28
BELGIUM
The last bits of the German "bulge" in the Ardennes are wiped out. The Germans have lost 100,000 killed, wounded, and captured in their defeat. The Americans have lost 81,000 killed, wounded, or captured, and the British 1,400 killed.

January 30
GERMANY
The Red Army is only 100 miles (160 km) from Berlin.

February 4–11
SOVIET UNION
Marshal Joseph Stalin, President Franklin D. Roosevelt, and Prime Minister Winston Churchill meet at the Yalta Conference in the Crimea to discuss postwar Europe. The "Big Three" decide that Germany will be divided into four zones, administered

TIMELINE

by Britain, France, the United States, and the Soviet Union.

FEBRUARY 13–14
GERMANY
The RAF mounts a night raid on Dresden. The 805 bombers inflict massive damage on the city, killing 50,000 people.

FEBRUARY 17
IWO JIMA
Under the command of Lieutenant General Holland M. Smith, the U.S. Marines land on the island of Iwo Jima. The attackers are hit by intense artillery and small-arms fire from the 21,000-man Japanese garrison.

MARCH 16
IWO JIMA
The island of Iwo Jima is declared secure by the Americans. They have lost 6,821 soldiers and sailors dead, while of the 21,000 Japanese garrison, only 1,083 are taken prisoner.

MARCH 22–31
GERMANY
The Allied crossings of the Rhine River begin. German resistance is negligible.

APRIL 1
OKINAWA
Operation Iceberg, the U.S. invasion of the island, commences. The island, only 325 miles (520 km) from Japan, has two airfields on the western side and two partially-protected bays on the east coast. It offers an excellent springboard for the proposed invasion of the Japanese mainland.

APRIL 7
PACIFIC OCEAN
The Japanese *Yamato*, the world's largest battleship, is sunk at sea during an attack by U.S. warplanes.

APRIL 9
ITALY
The final campaign in Italy begins as the U.S. Fifth and British Eighth Armies attack the Germans.

APRIL 12
UNITED STATES
President Franklin D. Roosevelt dies of a cerebral haemorrhage. Vice President Harry S. Truman takes over the position of president.

APRIL 16
GERMANY
The Soviet offensive to capture Berlin commences with a total of 2.5 million men, 41,600 guns and mortars, 6,250 tanks and self-propelled guns, and 7,500 combat aircraft. The Germans have one million men, 10,400 guns and mortars, 1,500 tanks or assault guns, and 3,300 combat aircraft.

APRIL 27
GERMANY
"Fortress Berlin" has been reduced to an east-to-west belt 10 miles (16 km) long by 3 miles (5 km) wide. German forces within the city are affected by widespread desertions and suicides.

APRIL 28
ITALY
Former Italian dictator Benito Mussolini and his mistress Claretta Petacci are captured by partisans. They are both shot.

APRIL 30
GERMANY
Adolf Hitler and Eva Braun commit suicide in the Führerbunker in Berlin.

MAY 2
GERMANY
Following a savage three-day battle in which half the garrison has been killed, Berlin, the capital of Nazi Germany, falls to the Red Army.

MAY 3
BURMA
Following 38 months of Japanese occupation, Rangoon falls to the Allies without a fight.

JUNE 22
OKINAWA
All Japanese resistance on the island ends. The Japanese have lost 110,00 killed during the fighting. The U.S. Tenth Army has suffered 7,613 men killed or missing and 31,807 wounded.

JULY 17–AUGUST 2
GERMANY
The Potsdam Conference takes place in Berlin. The "Big Three"—U.S. President Harry Truman, Soviet leader Marshal Joseph Stalin, and British Prime Minister Clement Attlee (who had defeated Churchill in a general election on July 5)—meet to discuss postwar policy. Japan is informed that an immediate surrender would result in the continued existence of its nation, but further resistance will lead to the "utter devastation of the Japanese homeland." This is a veiled reference to the use of atomic weapons against Japan itself.

AUGUST 6
JAPAN
The B-29 Superfortress *Enola Gay* drops an atomic bomb on the Japanese city of Hiroshima, killing 70,000 people and wounding 100,000.

AUGUST 9
MANCHURIA
A massive Soviet offensive by 1.5 million men begins against the Japanese Kwantung Army.

AUGUST 9
JAPAN
A second U.S. atomic bomb is dropped on Nagasaki. It kills 35,000 people and injures a further 60,000.

AUGUST 10
JAPAN
Following a conference during which the emperor voices his support for an immediate acceptance of the Potsdam Proclamation, Japan announces its willingness to surrender unconditionally.

AUGUST 23
MANCHURIA
The campaign in Manchuria ends in total Soviet victory. The Japanese have lost over 80,000 dead and 594,000 taken prisoner. Soviet losses are 8,000 men killed and 22,000 wounded. The Kwantung Army has been destroyed.

SEPTEMBER 2
ALLIES
Aboard the battleship *Missouri* in Tokyo Bay, Japanese officials sign the Instrument of Surrender, bringing World War II to a close.

GLOSSARY

advance A move forward by a military force.

Allies One of the two groups of combatants in the war. The main Allies were Britain, the Soviet Union, the United States, British Empire troops, and free forces from occupied nations.

Anschluss German word for union. Used to refer to the political union of Austria with Germany in 1938.

appeasement Not standing up to an enemy.

armistice A temporary halt in fighting agreed to by both sides.

armor A term referring to armored vehicles, such as tanks.

Axis One of the two groups of combatants in the war. The leading Axis powers were Germany, Italy, and Japan.

Blitzkrieg A German word meaning "lightning war." It referred to the tactic of rapid land advance supported by great airpower.

civil war A war between two opposing groups of citizens of the same country.

communist A violent fanatic who supports politically left wing or subversive causes.

dive-bomber A war plane that dives toward its target before releasing its bombs at low altitude.

division An army unit made up of 15,000 to 20,000 soldiers.

embargo An order to temporarily stop something, especially trading.

fascist A supporter of a strongly nationalistic and militaristic political party.

garrison A group of troops placed to defend a location.

Holocaust The systematic German campaign to exterminate millions of Jews and others.

infantry Soldiers who are trained to fight on foot, or in vehicles.

Nazi A member of Adolf Hitler's National Socialist German Workers' Party.

occupation The seizure and control of an area by military force.

offensive A planned military attack.

panzer German word for tank.

Polish Corridor A strip of land that separated Germany from German East Prussia. Given to Poland in the Treaty of Versailles to provide it with access to the Baltic Sea.

putsch German word for uprising.

rationing A system of limiting food and other supplies to ensure that everyone gets a similar amount.

Reichstag The German parliament.

strategy A detailed plan for achieving success.

strongpoint Any defensive position that has been strengthened to withstand an attack.

Swastika The official emblem of the Nazi party and the Third Reich.

treaty A formal agreement between two or more countries.

troops Groups of soldiers.

ultimatum A demand made by one country on another.

FURTHER READING

BOOKS

Adams, Simon. *World War II* (Eyewitness Books). Dorling Kindersley, 2004.

Corrigan, Jim. *Causes of World War II* (The Road to War: Causes of Conflicts). OTTN Publishing, 2005.

Crew, David F. *Hitler and the Nazis: A History in Documents* (Pages from History). Oxford University Press USA, 2006.

Cunningham, Kevin. *Joseph Stalin and the Soviet Union* (World Leaders). Morgan Reynolds Publishing, 2006.

Fitzgerald, Stephanie. *Kristallnacht, the Night of Broken Glass: Igniting the Nazi War Against Jews* (Snapshots in History). Compass Point Books, 2008.

Freeman, Charles. *Why Did the Rise of the Nazis Happen?* (Moments in History). Gareth Stevens Publishing, 2010.

Gedny, Mona. *The Story of the Great Depression* (Monumental Milestones). Mitchell Lane Publishers, 2005.

Harris, Nathaniel. *The Rise of Hitler* (Witness to History). Heinemann-Raintree, 2004.

Haugen, Brenda. *Joseph Stalin: Dictator of the Soviet Union* (Signature Lives). Compass Point Books, 2006.

Hynson, Colin. *World War II: A Primary Source History* (In Their Own Words). Gareth Stevens Publishing, 2005.

Rice, Earle. *Adolf Hitler and Nazi Germany*. Morgan Reynolds Publishing, 2005.

Rice, Earle. *Blitzkrieg! Hitler's Lightning War* (Monumental Milestones: Great Events of Modern Times). Mitchell Lane Publishers, 2007.

Roberts, Jeremy. *Benito Mussolini*. Lerner Publishing Group, 2005.

Vander Hook, Sue. *Adolf Hitler: German Dictator*. Abdo Publishing Company, 2011.

WEB SITES

Due to the changing nature of Internet links, Rosen Publishing had developed an online list of Web sites related to this subject. This site is updated regularly. Please use this link to access the list:

http://www.rosenlinks.com/WW2/Begin

INDEX

A
Anschluss 35, 37, 38
Anti-Comintern Pact 38
anti-semitism 27
Anzio 59
appeasement 38
Ardennes 59
Arnhem 59
Aryan 10
Attlee, Clement 60
Austria 35

B
Barbarossa, Operation 57
Beer Hall Putsch 11, 18
Berlin 60
Blitzkrieg 37, 50
Bismarck 57
Bolsheviks 7
Braun, Eva 13, 60
Britain, Battle of 57
Brownshirts 17, 20
Brüning, Heinrich 22

C
Chamberlain, Neville 34, 39, 42, 56
Churchill, Winston 56, 59

D
D-Day 59
Dachau 25
Danzig 42, 51

Dollfuss, Engelbert 35
Dresden 60
Dunkirk 56
Dutch East Indies 58
Dynamo, Operation 56, 57

E
El Alamein, Battle of 58
Enola Gay 60

F
Fascism 12
"Final Solution" 57, 58
Franco, Francisco 37
Freikorps 8

G
German Communist Party 16, 23, 25
German Labor Front 30
German-Soviet Nonaggression Pact 53
German Workers' Party 16
Göring, Hermann 25, 26
Graf Spee 56
Great Depression 21
Guadalcanal 58

H
"Happy Time" 57
Henlein, Konrad 38
Heydrich, Reinhard 58
Himmler, Heinrich 26, 28

Hindenburg, Paul von 23
Hiroshima 60
Hitler, Adolf 4, 6, 7, 8, 11, 13, 14, 17, 18, 20, 21, 22, 23, 26, 27, 28, 29, 34, 36, 38, 41, 44, 47, 55, 58, 59, 60
Hitler, Alois 7
Hitler, Paula 6
Hitler Youth 31
Holocaust 29
Hood 57

I
Iceberg, Operation 60
Imphal 59
Iron Cross 8
Iwo Jima 60

K
Kasserine Pass, Battle of 58
Katyn Wood 55
Kiev 59
Kohima 59
Kurile Islands 58
Kursk, Battle of 58
Kwantung Army 60

L
League of Nations 10, 34
Lend-Lease Act 57
Lenin, Vladimir 7
Leyte Gulf, Battle of 59

63

INDEX

Locarno Treaty 20, 36
Luftwaffe 50, 52, 57

M

Market Garden, Operation 59
Marx, Karl 7
Marxists 10
Mein Kampf 12, 13, 18
Midway, Battle of 58
Molotov Cocktails 56
Monte Cassino 59
Munich Agreement 41
Munich Conference 34
Mussolini, Benito 17, 34, 42, 60

N

Nagasaki 60
National Socialist German Workers' Party 9, 16, 17, 25
Nazi Party 4, 10
Night of Broken Glass 29
Night of the Long Knives 26
North Cape, Battle of 59
Nuremberg Laws 27

O

Okinawa 60

P

Pearl Harbor 58
Pétain, Henri-Philippe 57
Philippine Sea, Battle of 59
Polish Corridor 44
Polish Home Army 59

Potsdam Conference 60
Prince Eugen 57
Prince of Wales 57

R

Raeder, Erich 36
Rangoon 60
Rathenau, Walther 16
Raubal, Geli 13
Reichstag 22
Rhineland 35
Ribbentrop Joachim von 47
River Plate, Battle of 56
Rommel, Erwin 57
Roosevelt, Franklin D. 56, 57, 59, 60
Royal Air Force 57

S

Schirach, Baldur von 31
Schleicher, Kurt von 23
Schutzstaffel 22, 57
Sevastopol 58
Seyss-Inquart, Arthur 38
Sicily 58
Singapore 58
Smolensk 59
Social Democrats 22
Spartacus League 16
Stalin, Joseph 41, 45, 53, 55, 59, 60
Stalingrad 58
Strasser, Gregor 12
Strength Through Joy 30
Stuka dive-bomber 50

Sudetenland 38, 41
Swastika 10

T

Taranto, Battle of 57
Tobruk 58
Treaty of Moscow 56
Truman, Harry S. 60
Typhoon, Operation 57

V

Versailles Treaty 18, 20, 21, 34, 36
Vienna 6

W

Wansee Conference 58
Warsaw 55
Warsaw Ghetto 58
Watch on the Rhine, Operation 59
Weimar Republic 16
Western Desert Force 57
Western Front 9
Wilhelm, Kaiser 16
Winter War 56

Y

Yalta Conference 59
Yamato 60
Young Plan 20